HIGH BALLS LONG BALLS & NO BALLS

HIGH BALLS LONG BALLS & NO BALLS

MIKE KIELY

ARCTURUS

ARCTURUS

This edition published in 2009 by Arcturus Publishing Limited
26/27 Bickels Yard, 151–153 Bermondsey Street,
London SE1 3HA

ISBN: 978-1-84837-370-9
AD001255EN

Illustrations by David Mostyn; cover photograph Corbis

Printed in Singapore

CONTENTS

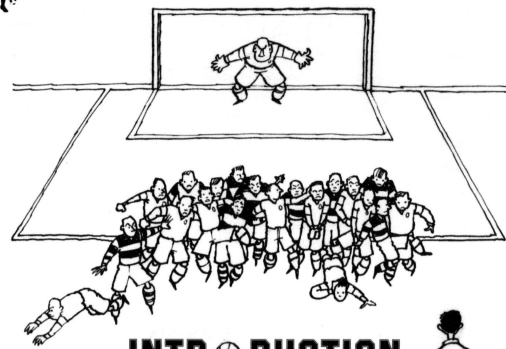

INTR⚽DUCTION

Much is said about football. According to Gary Lineker, '[it] is a very simple game. For 90 minutes 22 men go running after the ball and then the Germans win.' JB Priestly put it differently, 'To think of football as merely 22 hirelings kicking a ball is merely to say that a violin is wood and cat-gut, *Hamlet* so much ink and paper. It is conflict and art.' Jimmy Greaves was less lofty, merely observing, 'It's a funny old game.' One thing is certain: people will never run out of things to say about what's happening on and off the pitch. What follows is our selection of the good, the bad and the ugly.

ARSENAL

'For me Arsenal is a club which tries to respect tradition, style, honesty, fair play. If you come in and behave like a gangster you will not last long. The supporters will be the first ones not happy with that. A club needs values. If a club has no values you go nowhere.' ARSENE WENGER

'A football team is like a beautiful woman. When you do not tell her, she forgets she is beautiful.'
ARSENE WENGER

'To me, he will always be the Romford Pele.'
MARC OVERMARS on Ray Parlour

'That Seaman is a handsome young man, but he spends too much time looking in his mirror, rather than at the ball. You can't keep goal with hair like that.'
BRIAN CLOUGH on David Seaman

'The kid can run through puddles and not make a splash.'
HARRY REDKNAPP on the rare pace of Theo Walcott

'We do not buy superstars, we make them.'
ARSENE WENGER

'I've got a great photo at home of me at Selhurst Park. It's in three stages, and I'm going mad at the referee, and my face – I look at it and think, "Jesus Christ, I don't know that person. What is going on in his life?" It's quite frightening. I keep it in case I'm ever tempted to change my ways.' TONY ADAMS

'Hearing my name chanted on the North Bank just a couple of years after standing there chanting names myself, that was better than sex. Not that I can remember much about sex.'

CHARLIE GEORGE

'I would not normally say this as a family man, but I am going to ask you, for your sakes and for the sake of this football club, to put your family second for the next month. You have the chance to put your names in the record books for all time.'

BERTIE MEE rallies his troops for the run-in to the double in 1971

'That was the longest three minutes I have ever known.'

RAY KENNEDY on holding on to clinch the title at White Hart Lane in 1971

'I always thought playing with Wrighty was the most exhilarating experience anyone could have. He was really off the cuff, no one knew what he was going to do – I think Ian didn't know half the time.'

LEE DIXON on Ian Wright

'Those that say it is the taking part and not the winning that is important are, for me, wrong. It is the other way round.'
TONY ADAMS

'He should have been prime minister. He might have been but for the lack of opportunities entailed by his position in the social scale.'
CLIFF BASTIN on Herbert Chapman, who won two league titles and the FA Cup with Arsenal in the 1930s

'When I look back at my time managing Arsenal in the '80s, I wonder how much more we could have achieved had my team not been boozing so much.'
GEORGE GRAHAM

'I've never been a goalscorer, only own goals. Good own goals.'
STEVE BOULD

'We arrived at the hotel half an hour early. Chapman immediately went into the lounge bar. He called the waiter, placed two pound notes in his hand and said, "George, this is Mr Wall, my assistant. He will drink whisky and dry ginger. I will drink gin and tonic. We shall be joined by guests. They will drink whatever they like. See that our guests are given double of everything, but Mr Wall's whisky and dry ginger will contain no whisky, and my gin and tonic will contain no gin."'
BOB WALL, Herbert Chapman's assistant, on how his boss left nothing to chance during the transfer negotiations for striker David Jack in 1928. As Bolton Wanderers' officials 'relaxed', the price went down from £13,000 to £10,890, which was still a record

'Some rich men like to buy fast cars, yachts or racehorses. But David is more interested in Arsenal. I'm delighted he is – but I still think he's crazy. To all intents and purposes, it's dead money.'

PETER HILL-WOOD on David Dein's investment in Arsenal, 1983. In 2007, Dein sold his shares to Red & White Holdings for £75m – he bought his original holding for £292,000

'There's no chance of Sol leaving for Arsenal. He is a Spurs fan and there's not a hope in hell of him playing in an Arsenal shirt.'

DAVID BUCHLER, Tottenham chairman

'Well, I won't be picking it for a while!'

ANDY LINIGHAN on the broken nose he suffered in the 1993 FA Cup Final replay when he nodded in the winner

'When the ball bounced off me it could have gone anywhere, but it just fell perfectly for him. How do you explain that? You can't, except to say that things happen.'

Liverpool defender STEVE NICOL on Michael Thomas' last gasp title-winning goal at Anfield in 1989

'Most of them are investment people and they are not buying into clubs because they have the passion for the local team they have supported since they were two years old.'

PETER HILL-WOOD on foreign ownership of English clubs

'He was an adventurous player, and the fans absolutely loved him.'
PAUL DAVIS remembers David Rocastle, who died of cancer at the age of 33

'Commentator: "That's 1–0 to the Arsenal." George Allison: "And that's just the way we like it."'
Dialogue from the film, *The Arsenal Stadium Mystery* (1939)

'There was no right time to sell Patrick Vieira. What's important now is to show great strength and togetherness.'
ARSENE WENGER

'Pat Rice and I were in the centre circle discussing who'd go next. I said, "Go on, take some responsibility." Pat replied, "No. It's you next." But as he said it Rix missed, so we didn't need to decide.'
SAMMY NELSON on the penalty shootout in the 1980 Cup Winners' Cup final

'When I watch Arsenal on television I get so tense I sometimes have to leave the room.'
SAMMY NELSON

'Alan was a master with both Arsenal and England. He said to me, "When I get the ball, Mal, you get on your bike. If I don't deliver it with my first touch I will with my second. I never take three touches." He was as good as his word, a real inspiration.' MALCOLM MACDONALD on Alan Ball

ASTON VILLA

'There's an aura about this club, a sense of history and tradition. Even the name is beautifully symmetrical, with five letters in each word.' JOHN GREGORY

'Here he is, the one who cost us a place in the final.'

GARETH SOUTHGATE has to take the banter on the chin after missing the decisive penalty against Germany in Euro 96

'I put my arms round him, gave him a big kiss, and then cried my eyes out. Honestly. I loved being manager of Aston Villa. But I just felt that I was banging my head against a brick wall. It was time to move on while things were still pretty cool.'
JOHN GREGORY on saying goodbye to 'Deadly' Doug Ellis

'I told him I'd sooner have him in front of me where I could see him.'
TOMMY DOCHERTY on being told by Doug Ellis he was right behind him

'Once Ashley puts some weight on he will be fantastic. At the moment he's about three and a half stone – a couple of times we have put him through the letterbox!'
MARTIN O'NEILL on Ashley Young

'Martin O'Neill, standing, hands on hips, stroking his chin.'
MIKE INGHAM

'People have opinions, but I've got to make judgements, and there's a world of difference.'
MARTIN O'NEILL

'I'd like to play for an Italian club, like Barcelona.'
Midfielder MARK DRAPER

'We lived the dream in 1981 and 1982 and since then the club has struggled to emulate those times.'
DENNIS MORTIMER

'The hardest part of captaining that team was tossing the coin and picking up the trophies.'
DENNIS MORTIMER

'I felt I was being used as a tool in a political boxing match and I found that very disconcerting.'
DAVID JAMES on internal problems in 2000

'One morning, in December 2000, someone called me and said, "Have you seen he has called you Mr Blobby?" It was hard to cope with that because I've always looked after myself. I took it personally. If you tell a footballer he is overweight you are saying that he is not serious in his life and not thinking about football in the right way.'
DAVID GINOLA responds to the words of John Gregory

'Very few of us have any idea whatsoever of what life is like living in a goldfish bowl – except, of course, for those of us who are goldfish.'
GRAHAM TAYLOR

'You couldn't pass water.'

RON SAUNDERS keeps Gordon Cowan's feet on the ground

'Do you want to bet against us?'
RON SAUNDERS throws the gauntlet down to the press after Villa slip up before eventually winning the 1981 First Division title

'It was scandalous. What had I done to deserve that? Nothing.'
HARRY REDKNAPP is given a hot reception at Villa Park

'Brian Little was my best pal; he had long hair and was well into music like me. I used to think he was on pills, given the way he'd dance. Look at him now, a sensible manager with a sensible haircut.'
JOHN GIDMAN

'I congratulate Martin O'Neill. He's done a great job since he arrived. Thank God I signed him before I left.'
DOUG ELLIS

BACKROOM STAFF

'I might go into the dressing room before a game with my picture of Jackie Milburn holding his medals. I'd say to the players, "Get your finger out, look what he won for £20 a week."'

KATH CASSIDY, tea lady at St James' Park for over 40 years, with her ideas on how to help Alan Shearer to avoid relegation

---

'Would you leave your home like that?'

St Johnstone tea lady AGGIE MOFFATT takes Graeme Souness to task over an untidy dressing room when he was Rangers manager

'I thought I had died and gone to heaven when I heard the news he was coming back. I still remembered that he takes one and a half sugars.'

KATH CASSIDY on the return of Kevin Keegan

'The kit man is staying. He's up for the battle. And the tea lady.'

Portsmouth manager TONY ADAMS laughs off player departures from Fratton Park during the January 2009 transfer window

'There are dead patches and it looks like dozens of cricket batting strips in a nice green outfield.'

Groundsman MATTHEW FROST bemoans the state of the pitch at the Luzhniki stadium ahead of the 2008 Champions League final between Chelsea and Manchester United

'The missus gets fed up with it. We went to Santa Ponsa [Mallorca] on holiday when I was working at the JJB Stadium, and on the way to our hotel passed a smart little football stadium. As soon as I got the chance, I had a walk down there to see what I could get from the groundsmen.' Old Trafford groundsman KEITH PORTER on his busman's holiday

'When they come here they get put right in the picture. I could name a few who've been a pain in the backside, but I don't like to give secrets away.'

Everton kitman JIMMY MARTIN on his no-nonsense approach

'Let's hope it's lucky thirteenth.'
Newcastle United tea lady KATH CASSIDY on Graeme Souness, the 13th manager she has served at the club

'Brian Little just had a rusty bag of tools to work with this year.'
Racecourse ground turnstile operator NEIL COOKE on Wrexham's relegation from the football league

'The most educated person at Real Madrid is the woman who cleans the toilets.'
JOAN GASPART, Barcelona vice-president

'Grass grows by the inch and is destroyed by the foot.'
PHIL COLLINSON, Rochdale groundsman

'The last time I saw a goal like that was in schoolboy football. The ball hardly had enough pace to get over the goal-line if it had not pitched up.'
ROY HODGSON berates Blackburn groundsman Steve Patrick after the ball hits a divot and flies past Tim Flowers

BECKHAM

'The way I and my family have been treated is an absolute disgrace. At the end of the day, I'm a nice person and loving husband and father. I've been called a bad father, I've been called a bad husband, and my wife has been called a bad mother. Things always hurt that are said about my family, and for people to call my wife a bad mother is unbelievable. I'm a strong person, I'm a strong family man, I'm a strong husband and a strong father.'

'My wife picked me out of a football sticker album, and I chose her from a music video.'

'This is what I do when I'm bored: new tattoos, new cars, new watches.'

'People love me because of football. To me, merchandising is an extra and derives from the fact that I'm a footballer.'

'I'm not the best talker, not at least until I know someone well.'

'I always used to go for blondes and quiet girls, but Victoria is the total opposite – dark and loud.'

'I was so nervous about doing that campaign because obviously I've done photo shoots before, but I've never done photo shoots in my underwear. When the photos first came out, my mother was the first one to call me and say, "What are you doing?" I tried explaining it to her, but she didn't really get it. Luckily, I've not been in the car with her when we've driven past one of the billboards.'

'It's not easy when someone pulls your ponytail.'

'When they picked teams at school, I was always the last chosen.'

'I like nice clothes, whether they're dodgy or not.'

'I remember so clearly us going into hospital so Victoria could have Brooklyn. I was eating a Lion bar at the time.'

'When people talk to me about being a gay icon I think of it as a great honour.'

'I have come to accept that if I have a new haircut it is front page news. But having a picture of my foot on the front page of a national newspaper is a bit exceptional.'

'People go on about my foul on Simeone and the red card but I'd obviously rather people talk about me scoring the penalty [against Argentina] four years later.'

'Whether it's men or women who fancy you, it's nice to be liked.'

'Alex Ferguson is the best manager I've ever had at this level. Well, he's the only manager I've actually had at this level. But he's the best manager I've ever had.'

'My parents have been there for me, ever since I was about 7.'

'I'm sure some people think I've not got the brains to be that clever, but I do.'

On the controversy after he was accused of deliberately getting a yellow card against Wales

'I definitely want Brooklyn to be christened, but I don't know into what religion yet.'

'Having been captain for 58 of my 95 caps I feel the time is right to pass on the armband as we enter a new era under Steve McClaren. I want to stress that I wish to continue to play for England and look forward to helping both the new captain and Steve McClaren in any way I can.'

'At home things are hard. For instance, my curtains are never open, I get no privacy at all. In fact, I can't remember the last time I saw daylight in my house.'

'We've been asked to do Playboy together, me and Victoria, as a pair. I don't think I'll ever go naked, but I'll never say never.'

'I dream a lot about football and a lot of them have come true for me.'

'Pele was a complete player. I didn't see him live obviously, because I wasn't born.'

'Well, I can play in the centre, on the right and occasionally on the left side.'
On his 'volatility' as a player

'I've got more clothes than Victoria.'

'*I feel like a piece of meat.*'

'*I like Victoria for herself, not for nothing else. I'd like her if she worked in Tesco.*'

'*I find it very similar to Manchester. [Milan] has that tradition that only big clubs have. At Milan, as at United, there is a special atmosphere, at the training ground, the stadium. Then Milan has a great trophy room.*'

'*People react to criticism in different ways, and my way is definitely to come out fighting.*'

'*He said, "You're one of the casualties." There was no shouting, no crying. Not on the phone to the manager anyway.*'

On being told by new England coach Steve McClaren he was out of the squad

'*It's amazing, being married to Victoria, because I'm in love with her... and I can also go into her room and use all the body creams and facial creams.*'

'*I can totally understand the way the manager thought. When you're a footballer, traditionally all you're meant to think about is football, but I need other things outside of football as well.*'

On manager Sir Alex Ferguson's dislike of his extra-curricular appearances.

'*Funny stalkers, scary stalkers, every kind of stalker.*'

On the downside of life in Madrid

'*My feelings for Manchester, the club, the players, the fans and staff, are as strong as ever.*'

'*I always wanted to be a hairdresser.*'

BIG HITTERS

'I want to help other clubs. I speak my mind and other chairmen should too. In fact, they can come and have lunch with me at Harrods, where I can serve them stags' testicles from my Scottish estate, Balnagowan. We all need big balls in this business.' MOHAMED AL FAYED, chairman of Fulham

'Let the women play in more feminine clothes like they do in volleyball. They could, for example, have tighter shorts.'

Fifa president SEPP BLATTER on 'improvements' to the women's game

'Let's talk about football and women. [Turning to four-times-married German Chancellor, Gerhard Schroeder.] Gerhard, why don't you start?'
SILVIO BERLUSCONI

'Football hooligans? Well, there are 92 club chairmen for a start.'
BRIAN CLOUGH

'We can't behave like crocodiles and cry over spilt milk and broken eggs.'
GIOVANNI TRAPPATONI

'Lombardo speaks much better English than what people realize.'
MARK GOLDBERG, Crystal Palace chairman, on his new Italian acquisition

'I do not think there should be criticism of TV. It is the rocket fuel that sent the Premier League into the stratosphere.'

RICHARD SCUDAMORE, Premier League chief executive

'Me and Joe [Kinnear] are so close we will continue living in the same underpants.'

Wimbledon chairman SAM HAMMAM on his manager

'We have made an undertaking to Arsene Wenger and his family not to name our new coach.'

PETER HILL-WOOD, Arsenal chairman, failing to keep mum

'We have one prime minister for Thailand going back to his country and he sells his club like you would sell a shirt.'

SEPP BLATTER on Thaksin Shinawatra's sale of Manchester City to the Abu Dhabi United Group

'I do not like the system of Arsene Wenger. In France, Italy and Spain it is easy to buy with money the best players at 14, 15 or 16. I don't like that.'

MICHEL PLATINI

'It would be useful to remind people that slaves in all of the slavery systems never earned a wage.'

Uefa communications director WILLIAM GAILLARD responds to Sepp Blatter's description of footballers' contracts as 'modern slavery'

'I see other clubs' chairmen as the enemy.'

SIMON JORDAN, Crystal Palace chairman

'I would be criticized wholly if we let the league stray into the slow lane while others passed us in the fast lane. We have to do something.'

RICHARD SCUDAMORE, Premier League chief executive, on proposals to play matches outside the UK

'Soon in England you will have no English players, no English managers, just foreign speculators.'

MICHEL PLATINI

'The invaluable jewel is a world-class player born within striking distance of your local stadium. Steven Gerrard at Liverpool and John Terry at Chelsea is what every club aspires to. But they are becoming rarer. But it's also down to the player's character. Arsenal fans will say they got loyalty from Dennis Bergkamp. Chelsea fans will say they got loyalty from Gianfranco Zola, who played longer for Chelsea than Alan Hudson.'

RICHARD SCUDAMORE, Premier League chief executive, on foreign players

BIRMINGHAM CITY

'The Birmingham people are working class and they saw themselves in me. Most of the fans probably had more ability than me, but they saw someone prepared to run for the cause and they appreciated that.' ROBBIE SAVAGE

'We've got to learn to compete. It's no use standing around because the shirt won't run about by itself.'

BARRY FRY

'I asked Sir Alex about Birmingham before I took the job, and he thought it was a good club, a proper old-fashioned English club, with fervent support. He felt it would be a good platform for me.'

ALEX McLEISH receives the green light from Sir Alex Ferguson

'We went down that season, but a year later – after he'd gone home and we'd come back up – I met him at Wembley. "Boss!" he shouts. "We had crap team. Now you good team. Why not me with you?"'

JIM SMITH remembers Alberto Tarantini and season 1978/79

'I was watching the Blackburn game on TV when it flashed on the screen that George [Ndah] had scored in the first minute at Birmingham. My first reaction was to ring him up. Then I remembered he was playing.'
ADE AKINBIYI

'I love Birmingham City. I wish I could go back one day and have the recognition I deserve, but I know that will never happen because of my big mouth.'
ROBBIE SAVAGE

'I didn't want him anywhere near my team.'
STEVE BRUCE vetoes the arrival of Hossam Ghaly from Spurs after the Egyptian complained about his training methods

'There is no better player in the country than Trevor Francis.'
SIR ALF RAMSEY

'Keep Right On To The End of The Road'

The title of HARRY LAUDER's famous music hall anthem adopted by Blues fans during the 1956 FA Cup run

'When there's a large chunk of your supporters singing, "Sack the board" and shouting at me, in front of my kids, "F*** off, you little ******", you think to yourself, "What am I doing here?"'
Plc chairman DAVID SULLIVAN on the supporters' reaction to relegation

BIG RON

'I think Sir Alex might have been thinking about pulling Giggsy off... but that might be an incentive to stay on.'

'Moreno thought that the full-back was gonna come up behind and give him one really hard.'

'The Spaniards have been reduced to aiming aimless balls into the box.'

'Well, either side could win it, or it could be a draw.'

'Suker – first touch like a camel.'

'If that's Junior Biano, I wouldn't like to meet Senior Biano.'

'There's a little triangle – five left-footed players.'

'There's lots of balls dropping off people.'

'For me their biggest threat is when they get into the attacking part of the field.'

'Well, Clive, it's all about the two Ms
– Movement and Positioning.'

'When Scholes gets it [tackling]
wrong, they come in so late that
they arrive yesterday.'

'Liverpool are outnumbered
numerically in midfield.'

'I would also think that the replay
showed it to be worse than it
actually was.'

'He's not only a good player, but
he's spiteful in the nicest sense
of the word.'

'You half fancied that to go in. It was
rising and dipping at the same time.'

'Every time Zidane comes inside,
Roberto Carlos just goes bonking
down the wing.'

'You can see the ball go past them, or the man, but you'll never see both man and ball go past at the same time. So if the ball goes past, the man won't, or if the man goes past they'll take the ball.'

'He dribbles a lot and the opposition
don't like it – you can see it all over
their faces.'

BLACKBURN ROVERS

'It's acknowledged that we pick up more cards than anybody else and it's something we have to live with.' **MARK 'SPARKY' HUGHES**

'The SAS.'

TABLOID NICKNAME for the Shearer-Sutton strike partnership which helped Blackburn to the Premiership title in 1994/95

'Eyal is a professional and clearly wants to earn as much money as possible. But he is Jewish and I am Scottish so it will be difficult for us to reach a financial agreement.'

GRAEME SOUNESS on the possibility of Israeli Eyal Berkovic permanently joining Blackburn

'I am happy to be a role model for anybody – whether they are black, white, yellow, pink or purple.'

PAUL INCE on being appointed the Premiership's first black manager

'I was hugely disappointed by those gestures. I think they were disrespectful and quite humiliating. You don't expect those sort of things to happen in a game of football. I was very, very upset by it.'

SAM ALLARDYCE on Rafa Benitez's dismissive gestures during a 4–0 win by Liverpool

'He can be a little wayward but hopefully I'll be able to control him, as I did at Bolton.'

SAM ALLARDYCE on the acquisition of El-Hadj Diouf

BOLTON WANDERERS

'He [Megson] really likes his tactical work, but it is always based around the same gameplan – sending the ball up to Kevin Davies, who is very good in the air.' SEBASTIEN PUYGRENIER

'When Kevin came to the club he was somewhat a broken man but he had a good pre-season and then a good start. His confidence kicked in and everything fell into place for him quite nicely.'

PHIL BROWN on Kevin Davies

'There are scientists who will tell you that spirit, because it can't be measured, doesn't exist. Bollocks. It does exist.'
SAM ALLARDYCE imagines a breed of scientist that may or may not exist

'To be on the receiving end of that is probably the worst thing that can happen to you. It's something that nobody wants to see in football and I'm not going to sit here and try and defend it.'
Bolton midfielder GARY SPEED on an incident involving team-mate El-Hadj Diouf, who spat at Arjan de Zeeuw

'We are going to need a double-decker in front of our goal rather than the team coach!'
SAM ALLARDYCE reminds Jose Mourinho's Chelsea what awaits them at the Reebok

BRITISH PLAYERS ABROAD

'I loved the lifestyle, and the Nou Camp is an amazing place. The atmosphere for matches against Real Madrid was unlike anything I'd ever seen. I scored two goals in the opening five minutes of my first game against them and went on to get a hat-trick in a 3–2 win. It was the most blood-tingling experience of my life.'

GARY LINEKER on Barcelona

'Ruud Gullit, Marco van Basten, Frank Rijkaard, Paolo Maldini and Franco Baresi. And they all played in the same team! I remember playing them once and we went 1–0 up after 10 minutes. I thought, "This is good, we should be all right here." I didn't get another touch of the ball for 80 minutes and we lost 5–1. We were demolished. That team was frightening.'

PAUL GASCOIGNE on facing AC Milan

'Meals out were great, there was none of this having to book and wait for your wife to get ready. It was spontaneous.'

DAVID PLATT

'Playing with Pisa made me realize the universal problem with racism: the banana-throwing, the monkey-chanting and the booing. It was nasty, there was no doubt about that.'

PAUL ELLIOTT

'I'd say to people, "Well, even if I don't win anything here, I'll have played for one of the biggest clubs in the world alongside some of the biggest players in the world, and had an amazing experience." All that might have been true but I was lying, wasn't I?'
DAVID BECKHAM on Real winning La Liga in 2007

'I think I went on a run where I scored for seven games on the spin. Then in the next game I didn't score for 55 minutes and I was taken off. I was on the bench for the next game.'
MICHAEL OWEN on Real Madrid

'When it was 2–0, Souness amused himself by making fun of us with words and gestures. He may be a great player, but he isn't worth much as a man.'
Roma's DARIO BONETTI on facing Graeme Souness of Sampdoria

'If you told the normal British player there would be no sex or booze for three weeks, he'd be knocking the doors down.'

LIAM BRADY on enforced solitude during match preparations with Juventus

---

'I had no language, I had no car, I had a house with a fantastic fireplace, but I needed logs and I didn't know how to get logs. I'd see these logs piled up outside people's houses but I had no idea how to ask where they came from. I got so desperate I was walking around thinking about nicking some.'
MARK HUGHES on life at Barcelona

'They took to me because of my hard work and my attitude, I think. And it happened right from the start. It felt like I had their support all the way through the four years, not just when we were winning but through the difficult times as well.'

DAVID BECKHAM on the fans at Real Madrid

'I loved the country, the people, the food – all of it except the football, which was awful. It was far too defensive.'
DENIS LAW
on Italy

'He constantly worked on the team shape and each segment of the team also had separate coaches. Your running was strictly timed and all that sort of thing. It was completely different to Liverpool, where all we did was five-a-sides.'

IAN RUSH on Juventus coach Dino Zoff

'I was sent off in my first game. That went down well with the ultras, for a start.'

MARK HATELEY on winning over Milan's fans

'My lowest weight in France was about 6lb lighter than I ever was in England, and it made a huge difference.'

TONY CASCARINO on the importance of diet

'They just seem to get more out of life than we do.'

DAVID PLATT on the Italians

'I did learn a bit of Japanese, enough to book a table for dinner and be generally polite, but not enough to hold a proper conversation.'

GARY LINEKER on playing in the J-League

'I know all of the little things that go into making a player happy. Munich taught me that. They were a million miles ahead of anything I had seen in terms of preparation. They understood what affected players.'

MARK HUGHES

'In England I often felt like a square peg in a round hole. I feel at home here. I laugh and cry at the same things as they do.'

MICHAEL ROBINSON on his decision to remain in Spain at the end of his playing career

'I wasn't the best, I had limitations, but my attitude took me to Manchester United, Barcelona, Bayern Munich and Chelsea; some of the top clubs in Europe.'

MARK HUGHES

'After one match I said to Marco Tardelli, "Let's go for a beer." I was ordering my third glass, and he said he'd have to go, he'd finished. I was amazed. I was just getting warmed up. I soon learnt that in Italy they don't go out drinking for the evening, not the way we do.'

LIAM BRADY

CELTIC

'What these players have to realize is that when you put on the Celtic jersey you're not playing for a football team, you're playing for a community and a cause.' Tommy Burns

'Every time we open a cupboard, a Celtic supporter falls out.'

BRITISH EMBASSY OFFICIAL in Lisbon, 1967

'John, you're immortal.'
BILL SHANKLY greets Jock Stein after the European Cup victory over Inter in 1967

'Better than Stanley Matthews.'
JOCK STEIN on pint-sized winger Jimmy 'Jinky' Johnstone

'The best place to defend is in the other team's penalty box.'
JOCK STEIN

'We work hard all week, but on a Saturday we get the day off to play football.'
BERTIE AULD

'The best fans on the continent.'
EL MUNDO DEPORTIVO on the Celtic support

'When I was young I would play Subbuteo with my friend. There was a squad with horizontal green and white lines. I was captivated by the colours of the shirt.'
PAOLO DI CANIO

'There are many things I want to do after I retire as a player, such as visiting hot springs in Japan with my family or growing tomatoes while being really selective about the types of soil I use.'
SHUNSUKE NAKAMURA

'You Scottish folk always mention that my dad played for Celtic. It's a blessing from the spirits.'
GILL SCOTT-HERON, whose father Giles Heron became the first black player to sign for Celtic in 1951

'Spurs was a very big part of my life, they gave me a chance, an experience at a big club and I owe them for that. But I tell you what, I'd walk to Glasgow today for a chance to play for Celtic one more time.'
Ramon Vega

'The Inter players looked like gods, not footballers. They were immaculate, there wasn't a hair out of place. They had so much glamour. Their blue and black tops had been hand-pressed by an expert. A lot of us were standing there minus our false teeth. It didn't look like a fair fight. I stared at Giacinto Facchetti, their world-famous left-back. At 6ft 3in, he was such an imposing figure. He looked as though he had stepped straight out of a sportswear catalogue. I turned round to wee Jimmy Johnstone and said, "Did he not go out with Sophia Loren?"'
BERTIE AULD on lining up against Inter in Lisbon in 1967

'Jock wouldn't suffer fools and if he felt anyone wasn't treating the game in the serious way he did, or that they were not following his instructions, he would let them know in no certain terms. Football was his religion, though, and he studied tactics as some would the Bible.' SEAN FALLON, Jock Stein's assistant

'He was a man with presence, and a man who you knew was a legend. Sometimes when you meet legends, you are a little disappointed – but that was never the case with Jock. When he walked into a room, the room filled with Jock Stein.'

GORDON STRACHAN

'Hugh Dallas still cannot believe he got struck by a £1 coin! Where did a Celtic fan get that kind of money?'
THE *DAILY RECORD* on a controversial moment during a stormy Old Firm match

'He says it has been a privilege being here, but the privilege was all ours.'
MARTIN O'NEILL on Henrik Larsson

'If he [Van Hooijdonk] offers me an olive branch, I'll stick it up his f***ing arse!'
DAVE BASSETT won't forgive the ex-Celt

'There was a lot of commitment in Celtic's game, commitment, toughness and aggression. I'm tempted to use another word – but I won't.'
Porto manager JOSE MOURINHO after his side's 3–2 defeat of Celtic

'Are there Martians out there?
I haven't got a clue. Is there life out
there? I have no idea.'
GORDON STRACHAN's left-field
response to transfer speculation

'Paul told me that's the first one
he's missed, which I find very
surprising having seen that.'
GORDON STRACHAN on a Paul Hartley
miss from the spot

'I had to know if I could make it
somewhere else. I did not want to
go through the rest of my life
wondering what might have been
without putting myself to the test.'
KENNY DALGLISH explains his decision
to leave for Liverpool in 1977

'He was born and brought up in the
Calton district of Glasgow – a
stone's throw from Celtic Park – and
he got to live the dream.'
DAVIE PROVAN pays tribute to
Tommy Burns

'Some clubs have dressing-room meetings if they lose three or four games, but at Celtic we did it if we lost at all.'
DAVID MOYES

'He is a complete individual. As far as assessing what is required for
Celtic he is intelligent, he has achieved, he understands football and he
understands footballers. He also understands value. There is an awful
lot to Martin O'Neill. The only person who could compete with Martin is
Alex Ferguson. I think Martin will prove that.'
DERMOT DESMOND on Martin O'Neill

'Just because we do not know the names of some of these teams from eastern Europe does not mean they are not any good.'

MURDO MACLEOD on the 5–0 defeat by Artmedia Petrzalka

'They wanted Kenny Dalglish, they didn't want me.'

JOHN BARNES
on his time as
Celtic manager

'I did have an affinity with Celtic, like any little Catholic boy in Ireland. When their great '67 team came to Dublin, I got their autographs.'
LIAM BRADY

'I was never obsessed with myself as a footballer, I just did things and that was it – I forgot about them and ordered the next drink.'
GEORGE CONNELLY on his alcoholism

'My first manager, Billy McNeill at Celtic, had such a presence that you almost stood to attention.'
DAVID MOYES

'There was a lot in the press about beards being banned there. It was a little intimidating, too, because when we went outside there were only men in the streets and no women to be seen.'
DANNY 'THE BEARD' McGRAIN on 1970s Albania

CHELSEA

'Money plays an important role in football but it is not the dominating factor. When Chelsea play a Carling Cup game in a small city and it could result in a draw – the excitement, the spirit, the atmosphere – that's the real beauty of football in England.' ROMAN ABRAMOVICH

'For John Terry, to die on the pitch would be glory. You would need to kill him – and maybe even then he'd still play on.'
'BIG PHIL' SCOLARI

'I would like to be Chelsea manager next season, why not?'
AVRAM GRANT

'If Chelsea drop points, the cat's out in the open. And you know what cats are like – sometimes they don't come home.'
ALEX FERGUSON

'Why have Chelsea suffered so much since I left? Because I left.'
JOSE MOURINHO

'That Cookie. When he sold you a dummy you had to pay to get back into the ground.'
JIM BAXTER on legendary winger Charlie Cook

CHELSEA

'Since I've had kids every penny I earn and every yard I run on the football pitch is for my kids.'

An emotional FRANK LAMPARD rebuts James O'Brien's criticisms live on LBC Radio

'You know Dennis Wise. He could start a fight in an empty house.'

ALEX FERGUSON

'Roman Abramovich has parked his Russian tanks on our lawn and is firing £50 notes at us.'
DAVID DEIN

'Drogba – the strength of a bull but the pain threshold of a lamb.'
CLIVE TYLDESLEY

'When Kenyon came, I was frozen [out].'
CLAUDIO RANIERI

'Gianfranco tries everything because he is a wizard and the wizard must try.'
GIANLUCA VIALLI

'95 per cent of my language problems are the fault of that stupid little midget Dennis Wise.'
GIANFRANCO ZOLA

'I'm the most local lad they've had in their history, but they don't treat you right. They're a Russian club now. They're not Chelsea Football Club.'
ALAN HUDSON

'Don't hoover up while Chelsea are playing because, if you knock the telly, Robben will fall over!'
RUUD GULLIT

'One is never 100 per cent motivated. In winter, when it's raining and you have to go and play a small team in the north, I won't reveal what passes through your mind when you're getting out of the bus.'
MARCEL DESAILLY

'If Chelsea are naive and pure then I'm Little Red Riding Hood.'
RAFA BENITEZ

'The people I worked with every day, people I played golf with, people I exchanged gifts with, these people were doing things behind my back... that was the worst thing.'
RUUD GULLIT on Chelsea politics

'There has been a clash of eastern and western cultures, and eastern and western values.'
KEN BATES leaves Chelsea

'It is born out of hypocrisy and fundamental insecurity. There have been two kids on the block for the past 12 years. Suddenly, there is a third and that one is threatening to be more successful than the others and they don't like it.'
PETER KENYON on criticism of Chelsea

'These days the Brits get outnumbered, but back then Chelsea was a very British club. Just look at the ground. When I started it was horrible, an absolute eyesore. There was the Shed but it wasn't pretty and it was so far from the pitch the supporters needed binoculars to see what was going on.' *FRANK SINCLAIR*

'We have eight matches and eight victories, with 16 goals, but people say we cannot play, that we are a group of clowns. This is not right.'

JOSE MOURINHO

'I'd have loved playing now because you know you can play football. There aren't gorillas kicking you. But in my day, if you moaned to the ref, your opponent would mutter, "Come on, you poof, get on with it."'

PETER OSGOOD

'Robbery With Violence.'

NEWSPAPER HEADLINE the morning after Chelsea defeated Leeds United 2–1 in the 1970 FA Cup final replay

'Talking more bollocks, are we, Ruud?'

DENNIS WISE interrupts an interview with the *Independent*, 1996

'It's best that I hide my real personality. I cannot tell you what it is because I don't want to go to prison.'

GIANFRANCO ZOLA

'When we get stick like that we're more determined than ever to shut them up.
We came to get three points and their fans walked away with nothing. You can't buy that.'

JOHN TERRY shows his pleasure on winning at Upton Park after a torrent of abuse from West Ham fans

'I have two season tickets to Chelsea, so I go whenever I can. The people I didn't get on with are no longer there, and I have a great relationship with the fans.'

GIANLUCA VIALLI

'Chelsea in their slightly unusual away colours – jade.'

Commentator JOHN MOTSON touches on a fashion faux pas from the 1980s

'I am a fan of special nature. I'm getting excited before every single game. The trophy at the end is less important than the process itself.'

ROMAN ABRAMOVICH

'At 14, I signed a two-year schoolboy form for Chelsea, and then it was a case of would I make it? I was playing in midfield and was really small – I was small and fat, basically. I think Chelsea were umming and aahing about my size, until all of a sudden, with perfect timing, I started shooting up. Then one day in the youth team we were struggling for centre-halves. So I played there and we won 3–0 and I've never looked back.'

JOHN TERRY

CLASSIC MOMENTS

'I'm still convinced it was over the line. I still stick to the same story. If you see it on TV now, you can see that I start to move in as Geoff hits a shot on the half volley. It hit the underside of the bar and I was only four yards away.'

ROGER HUNT on England's controversial third goal against West Germany in the 1966 World Cup final

'I remember the walk from the centre circle to the penalty spot being the longest in the world.'

GARETH SOUTHGATE recalls his penalty miss in the semi-final shoot-out of Euro 96

'Football – bloody hell.'

ALEX FERGUSON reacts to Manchester United's dramatic 2–1 victory over Bayern Munich in the 1999 Champions League final

'To beat the world champions on their own ground was mainly down to Jim Baxter.'

DENIS LAW remembers Scotland's 3–2 defeat of England at Wembley in 1967

'A brilliant individual goal by this hard little professional.'

DAVID COLEMAN describes Archie Gemmill's solo effort against Holland in the 1978 World Cup

'I have been living for the past 32 years with Banks in my memories.'
Brazil's JAIRZINHO on Gordon Banks

'The Greeks have made football history. It's a sensation.'
Coach OTTO REHHAGEL on the unlikely winners of Euro 2004

'That was sheer delightful football.'
KENNETH WOLSTENHOLME describes Carlo Alberto's goal and Brazil's fourth in the defeat of Italy in the final of the 1970 World Cup

'I lit up a huge cigar. It took me all night to smoke it! I am a big fan of American sports and that is what they do over there when they win. But I kept having to fire it up because I couldn't smoke the thing.'
Liverpool's VLADIMIR SMICER remembers the Champions League final in Istanbul

'Is Gascoigne going to have a crack? He is, you know. Oooh a goal! Brilliant. That is schoolboy's own stuff.'

BARRY DAVIES on Paul Gascoigne's free kick in the 1991 FA Cup semi-final against Arsenal

---

'I collapsed two or three more times in those last 15 minutes. I was in absolute agony and I was having to support my neck with my right hand. I couldn't move my head at all – if I wanted to look at anything, I had to turn my whole body around with my hand on my neck.'

Manchester City goalkeeper BERT TRAUTMANN plays on against Birmingham City in the 1956 FA Cup Final with what was later discovered to be a broken neck

---

'Venables tried to calm him down beforehand. We all did because he was so hyper. But, with Paul, he would listen and listen and agree with you and then, when he ran out on the pitch, he would forget everything and run at people like a dervish.'

GARY LINEKER on Paul Gascoigne prior to the 1991 FA Cup Final which ended with the midfielder being carried off with knee ligament damage after an impetuous tackle

'If you lose hope or lose belief, you may as well get out of football. Tonight was a fairytale, the unpredictable that makes us all love football.'

Manager GEORGE GRAHAM after a last-minute goal by Michael Thomas seals the title for Arsenal at Anfield in 1989

'As soon as I hit it I knew it was in, and I was off before it hit the back of the net.'

Hereford United's RONNIE RADFORD scores from 35 yards in the FA Cup third round against Newcastle United in 1972

'When Diego scored that second goal against us, I felt like applauding. I'd never felt like that before, but it's true... and not just because it was such an important game. It was impossible to score such a beautiful goal.'

GARY LINEKER remembers Diego Maradona's solo effort against England in the World Cup 1986 quarter-final

'That was a tough one to take. The sight of Mourinho dancing down the touchline was not a happy one for many people.'

JOHN O'SHEA after a last-minute goal by Porto knocked Manchester United out of the Champions League in 2004

'It's fabulous to score two goals in the final. There's nothing better – we're world champions.'
ZINEDINE ZIDANE in 1998

'Liverpool scored, if you can say that they scored, because maybe you should say the linesman scored.'
JOSE MOURINHO on Luis Garcia's disputed goal in 2005 that saw Liverpool defeat Chelsea in the Champions League semi-final

'It felt bloody heavy.'
BOBBY CHARLTON on what it was like to lift the European Cup for Manchester United in 1968

'Our plan was to be cautious, but somebody must have stuffed cotton wool in George's ears.'
MATT BUSBY on Manchester United's 5–1 European Cup victory over Benfica in 1966. George Best scored two goals

'Obviously, I was being clever. By letting myself fall, I got the referee to pull out a red card immediately.'

Argentina's DIEGO SIMEONE on David Beckham's red card at World Cup 98

'I was going to pass to a team-mate but I looked up and I saw Seaman coming out so I just kicked it. I was very lucky. It's my first goal against Arsenal after playing against them half a dozen times. For me it's something special as a former Tottenham player.'

NAYIM on his 45-yard lob over David Seaman that won the 1995 European Cup Winners' Cup for Real Zaragoza

'When the seagulls follow the trawler, it is because they think sardines will be thrown into the sea.' ERIC CANTONA

'It was a ridiculous bobble. For people to say it was an error and my fault was ridiculous.'

England goalkeeper PAUL ROBINSON on his air shot that resulted in a goal for Croatia in 2006

'The manager walked into the dressing room and said, "How can I slaughter you? You've just been part of one of the greatest games of all time."'
LES FERDINAND on Liverpool 4, Newcastle United 3 in 1996

'I didn't see it but sometimes football is not only with the ball.'
WILLIAM GALLAS reflects on Zinedine Zidane's headbutt on Marco Materazzi in the final of World Cup 2006

'They said, "Don't even bother going to Wembley. England will murder you."'
FERENC PUSKAS remembers a hostile Hungarian press ahead of England 3, Hungary 6 in 1953

'When Pele scored the fifth goal in that final, I have to be honest and say I felt like applauding.'
Sweden's SIGVARD PARLING remembers the defeat by Brazil in the 1958 World Cup final

CLICHÉS

'Our first goal was pure textile.'
JOHN LAMBIE

'I would not be bothered if we lost every game as long as we won the league.'
MARK VIDUKA

'He just walks into a room and a player grows by 20 per cent.'
Newcastle goalkeeper STEVE HARPER on Kevin Keegan

'No one hands you cups on a plate.'
TERRY McDERMOTT

'I promise results, not promises.'
JOHN BOND

'What I said to them at half time would be unprintable on the radio.'
GERRY FRANCIS

'I'm a firm believer that if the other side scores first you have to score twice to win.' HOWARD WILKINSON

'Klinsmann has taken to English football like a duck out of water.' GERRY FRANCIS

'What he's got is legs, which the other midfielders don't have.'
LENNIE LAWRENCE

'John Terry would run through a brick wall for Chelsea.'
RON HARRIS

'In terms of the Richter scale this was a Force 8 gale.'
JOHN LYALL

'And I honestly believe we can go all the way to Wembley – unless somebody knocks us out.'
DAVE BASSETT

'A lot of hard work went into this defeat.'
MALCOLM ALLISON

'An inch or two either side of the post and it would have been a goal.'
DAVE BASSETT

'Harry makes you feel ten feet tall. We went out on that pitch believing we were the greatest footballers who ever lived, whatever our ability.'
RIO FERDINAND on Harry Redknapp

'Hoddle hasn't been the Hoddle we know. Neither has Robson.'
RON GREENWOOD

'He taught me a new phrase because he said he was "over the moon" to be back.'
RAFAEL BENITEZ welcomes back Robbie Fowler to Anfield

CLOUGHIE

'I wouldn't say I was the best manager in the business. But I was in the top one.'

> '**I only ever hit Roy the once. He got up so I couldn't have hit him very hard.**'
>
> On coaching Roy Keane

'If God had wanted us to play football in the clouds, he'd have put grass up there.'

'We talk about it for 20 minutes and then we decide I was right.'
On man management

'Arsenal caress a football the way I dreamed of caressing Marilyn Monroe.'

'At last England have appointed a manager who speaks English better than the players.'
On Sven-Goran Eriksson

'Players lose you games, not tactics. There's so much crap talked about tactics by people who barely know how to win at dominoes.'

'I'm sure the England selectors thought if they took me on and gave me the job, I'd want to run the show. They were shrewd because that's exactly what I would have done.'

'They say Rome wasn't built in a day, but I wasn't on that particular job.'

'Manchester United in Brazil? I hope they all get bloody diarrhoea.'

Following the decision by United to forsake the FA Cup for the inaugural World Club Championship

'If a chairman sacks the manager he initially appointed, he should go as well.'

'I knew I was the best, but I should have said nowt and kept the pressure off 'cos they'd have worked it out for themselves.'

'I like my women to be feminine, not sliding into tackles and covered in mud.'

'Don't send me flowers when I'm dead. If you like me, send them while I'm alive.'

'The River Trent is lovely – I know because I have walked on it for 18 years.'

'Anybody who can do anything in Leicester but make a jumper has got to be a genius.'

On Leicester manager Martin O'Neill

'Walk on water? I know most people out there will be saying that instead of walking on it, I should have taken more of it with my drinks. They are absolutely right.'

'The ugliest player I ever signed was Kenny Burns.'

'Beckham? His wife can't sing and his barber can't cut hair.'

'On occasions I have been big-headed. I think most people are when they get in the limelight. I call myself Big Head just to remind myself not to be.'

COMMENTATORS

'People are on the pitch, they think it's all over. It is now, it's four. And the players fling themselves down.'

KENNETH WOLSTENHOLME, World Cup final, 1966

'Never go for a 50–50 ball unless you're 80–20 sure of winning it.'

IAN DARKE

'2–0 is a cricket score in Italian football.'

ALAN PARRY

'If that had gone in, it would have been a goal.'

DAVID COLEMAN

'If ever the Greeks needed a Trojan horse, it is now.'

GERALD SINSTADT

'England are sizzling in Shizuoka and after this the sausages will be sizzling back home.'

JOHN MOTSON

'Cantona's expression speaking the whole French dictionary without saying a word.'

BARRY DAVIES

'He went through a non-existent gap.'

CLIVE TYLDESLEY

'He's passing the ball like Idi Amin.'

ALAN PARRY

'The Crazy Gang have beaten the Culture Club.'

JOHN MOTSON, FA Cup Final, 1988

'It's going to take a shoehorn to prise these two teams apart.' ALAN PARRY

'Sporting Lisbon in their green and white hoops, looking like a team of zebras.'
PETER JONES

'Colour-wise, it's oranges v lemons, with the Dutch in all white.'
CLIVE TYLDESLEY

'52,000 here tonight, but it sounds like 50,000.'
BRYON BUTLER

'That's the kind he usually knocks in in his sleep, with his eyes closed.'
ARCHIE MACPHERSON

'I think this could be our best victory over Germany since the war.'
JOHN MOTSON

'As the seconds tick down, Belgium are literally playing in time that doesn't exist.'
GUY MOWBRAY

'The ageless Dennis Wise, now in his thirties.'
MARTIN TYLER

'A smoked salmon sandwich of a football match if ever there has been one.'
PETER DRURY

'I'm sure coach Frank Rijkaard will want the Dutch to go on and score a fourth now – although obviously they'll have to score the third one first.'
ANGUS LOUGHRAN

'Ziege hits it high for Heskey who isn't playing.'
ALAN GREEN

'Xavier, who looks just like Zeus, not that I have any idea what Zeus looks like.'
ALAN GREEN

'Chris Waddle is off the field at the moment, exactly the position he is at his most menacing.'
GERALD SINSTADT

'David O'Leary's poker face betrays the emotions.'
CLIVE TYLDESLEY

'It's Ipswich 0 Liverpool 2, and if that's the way the score stays then you've got to fancy Liverpool to win.'
PETER JONES

'It will be a shame if either side loses, and that applies to both sides.'
JOCK BROWN

'He had an eternity to play that ball, but he took too long over it.' MARTIN TYLER

ENGLAND

'I accept I made a serious error of judgement in an interview which caused misunderstanding and pain to a number of people. This was never my intention and for this I apologize.'

GLENN HODDLE is sacked in 1999 following comments about disabled people

'Argentina won't be at Euro 2000 because they're from South America.'

KEVIN KEEGAN

'Control yourself, Shephardson.'

ALF RAMSEY scolds assistant Harold Shepardson for leaping up when the final whistle blew to signal England had won the World Cup in 1966

'I used to quite like turnips. But now my wife refuses to serve them.'

GRAHAM TAYLOR references an English tabloid headline that likened his players to the root vegetable after defeat by the Swedes

'I could manage England part-time – and still walk the dog.'

BRIAN CLOUGH

'You know your mate's cost me my job?'

GRAHAM TAYLOR to a linesman about the referee of Holland v England in 1993

'We have nothing to learn from these people.'

SIR ALF RAMSEY, Guadalajara, 1970, after Brazil defeated England 1–0 with a goal from Jairzinho

'Being given chances and not taking them. That's what life is all about.'

RON GREENWOOD

'Look at Jesus. He was a normal, run-of-the-mill sort of guy who had a genuine gift.'

GLENN HODDLE

'If the pressure had frightened me I'd have kept my quality of life at Ipswich. I'd have kept driving my Jag six miles to work every day and got drunk with the chairman every Saturday evening.'

BOBBY ROBSON under pressure after England lost all three group games at the 1988 European Championships

'Michael Owen is a goalscorer – not a natural born one. Not yet, that takes time.'

GLENN HODDLE

'They called Puskas the "Galloping Major" because he was in the army – how could this guy serving for the Hungarian army come to Wembley and rifle us to defeat? But the way they played, their technical brilliance and expertise – our WM formation was kyboshed in 90 minutes of football.'

BOBBY ROBSON describes the shock of Hungary's 6–3 win over England in 1953, the national side's first loss at Wembley Stadium

'As soon as it dawned on me that we were short of players who combined skill and commitment, I should have forgotten all about trying to play more controlled, attractive football and settled for a real bastard of a team.'

DON REVIE reflects on his time with England

'I wouldn't say I'm a counter-attacking coach. I'm a find-a-way-to-win coach.'

STEVE McCLAREN

'Parker jumped like a salmon, tackled like a ferret.'
BOBBY ROBSON

'Do I not like that!'
GRAHAM TAYLOR during the 2–0 defeat to Norway

'There is no reason why we should be spoken about like Germany and Italy. It is an illusion. England have never been successful right back to the days of Matthews and Finney.'
TERRY VENABLES

'I know I asked for patience, but I didn't mean that much.'
SVEN-GORAN ERIKSSON after his side drew 2–2 with Greece to qualify for World Cup 2002, David Beckham scoring a decisive free kick in the very last minute

'A lot of my time is taken up with thinking adventurously.'
KEVIN KEEGAN

'You won't be surprised to know that I have some faith in astrologers and particularly what the stars predict for Scorpios.'
GLENN HODDLE

'If you want someone shouting, you will have to change the coach.'
SVEN-GORAN ERIKSSON

'We have still to produce our best football. It will come against a team who come to play football and not to act as animals.'
ALF RAMSEY after the controversial 1–0 quarter-final win over Argentina in 1966

'I drink tea every morning and in the afternoon. It's very nice! *Eastenders?* No, I don't watch that... but I'm sure it's very good.'
SVEN-GORAN ERIKSSON on the English lifestyle

'People think we don't give a toss about the game, but when I walked out of Windsor Park that night I felt lower than a snake's belly. No matter how much money you have or what kind of cocoon you live in, the reality is that you have lost a game of football and let England's fans down.'
RIO FERDINAND after defeat by Northern Ireland

'It was 1,000 per cent my decision. Please don't think anyone has put a gun to my head. I don't want to outstay my welcome... I have had all the help I have needed to do my job properly but I've not been quite good enough.'

KEVIN KEEGAN quits after losing 1–0 to Germany in the final match at the old Wembley Stadium, October 2000

'Gentlemen, if you want to write whatever you want to write, you can write it because that is all I am going to say. Thank you.'

STEVE McCLAREN addresses the press after Andorra 0 England 3

'We need goals when the scoreline is 0–0.'

SVEN-GORAN ERIKSSON

'England can end the millennium as it started – as the greatest football nation in the world.'

KEVIN KEEGAN ahead of Euro 2000

'What were you doing punching the corner flag? You're a crazy man, a crazy man.'

FABIO CAPELLO to Wayne Rooney

'I think in international football you have to be able to handle the ball.'

GLENN HODDLE

'I've worked for the last three England managers and seen what it did to them. I saw Ron Greenwood break out in sores, Bobby Robson go grey and poor Graham Taylor double up in anguish and stick his head so far between his legs that it nearly disappeared up his own backside.'

HOWARD WILKINSON, later to be caretaker manager, on the pressures involved in the England job

EVERTON

'Everton have always been noted for going out on the pitch to play football. We got called the School of Science quite rightly. The other lot, the Reds... well they were a gang of butchers!... they should have been working in an abattoir. God bless my soul! They'd kick an old woman.' DIXIE DEAN

'With Manchester City it was a love affair, but with Everton it's more like a marriage.'
HOWARD KENDALL

'I'd break every bone in my body for any club I play for, but I'd die for Everton.'
DAVE HICKSON

'I taught football to him not as a game, but as a way of life.'
ALAN BALL SENIOR on what he taught his son

'Ladies and gentlemen, today we are joined by a man who ranks amongst the greatest there is, Shakespeare, Rembrandt and Bach. This man is Dixie Dean.'
BILL SHANKLY on the former Everton centre forward

'One Blue is worth 20 Reds.'
Former centre back and captain
BRIAN LABONE

'Everton are the people's club in Liverpool. The people on the street support Everton.' DAVID MOYES

'I used to stick the ball in the net and bow three times to the Kop. They never liked me doing that.'

DIXIE DEAN

'I made my debut at Goodison against Stoke and was standing in the tunnel waiting to go onto the pitch. Z Cars started playing on the PA and I heard the crowd roar. If I could bottle a moment and save it forever, then that would be it.'

ALAN HARPER

'When I signed, I was told I was going to be the first of many big money signings. Someone was telling fibs.'

JOHN COLLINS remembers signing in at Goodison Park in 1999

'People keep on about stars and flair. As far as I'm concerned you find stars in the sky and flair at the bottom of your trousers.'

GORDON LEE

'The difference between Everton and the Queen Mary is that Everton carry more passengers.'

BILL SHANKLY

'If Everton finish in a Champions League place, they'll play in the Champions League.'
MARK BRIGHT

'Once a Blue, always a Blue.'
WAYNE ROONEY

'If you don't believe you can win, there is no point in getting out of bed at the end of the day.'
NEVILLE SOUTHALL

'Football was never the same for me after I left Everton and although I always wanted to win, losing never really seemed to hurt any more.'
KEVIN RATCLIFFE

'I soon got out of the habit of studying the top of the league.'
WALTER SMITH finds life at Everton somewhat different to Rangers

'Everton FC are really missing the loss of Arteta, and it's sticking out like a sore throat.'

former player turned pundit **RONNIE GOODLASS**

'I was running back to the centre circle after I scored the second goal against Liverpool and pure elation welled up inside me. I remember thinking, I just love this place – I want this place forever.'
ALAN BALL

'There's too much fantasy in this lad's story for one of my theatre shows. A boy who sits muttering in his monosyllabic way when the microphones are there can go out and bring 50,000 men to their feet in joy.'
Chairman BILL KENWRIGHT on Wayne Rooney

'We have to look after Wayne, and that includes every Evertonian. If you see him out in the street, send him home.'

DAVID MOYES on managing Wayne Rooney

'If anyone ever mentions the Everton School of Science to me again, well, I'm sorry, I just don't see it.'
Liverpool manager ROY EVANS

'Africa? We're not in bloody Africa, are we?'
GORDON LEE in Morocco

'Football is a bitch goddess.'
BILL KENWRIGHT

'TV just asked permission to interview Dunc. I said yes, but don't hold your breath. I'm just glad the refs can't understand a word he's saying to them.'
JOE ROYLE on Duncan Ferguson

'People ask me if that 60-goal record will ever be beaten. I think it will. But there's only one man who'll do it. That's that feller who walks on the water. I think he's about the only one.'
DIXIE DEAN

FANS

'This is a message for possibly the best supporters in the world. We need a twelfth man here. Where are you? Where are you? Let's be having you.'

Norwich City director DELIA SMITH gees up the home supporters against Manchester City

'When I think of the most important things in my life, there's my family first, then I've got boxing, next comes Manchester City, then it's Oasis.'

Boxer RICKY HATTON

'I relish the hostility from the fans, but they don't play.'
JOSE MOURINHO

'I'm on first-name terms with about half the crowd!'
JOHN McDERMOTT, defender at Grimsby Town, where the average attendance is just under 5,000

'It is incredible the passion with which Liverpool fans live their games. Even the smallest cup game has a great atmosphere there, it is as if they played with 12 men.'
Arsenal's CESC FABREGAS

'One young yobbo caught me. I think one of the security guards trod on him as he fell to the floor because I heard him squeal.'
NEIL WARNOCK after a close encounter with Bristol City fans

'When the match was over, a helicopter came down to whisk him off and I remember looking up and thinking, "I'll never see his like again."'

ALAN SHEARER remembers being on ball-boy duty for Kevin Keegan's last match in the black and white of Newcastle United

'Most of our fans get behind us and are fantastic, but those who don't should shut the hell up or they can come round to my house and I will fight them.'

IAN HOLLOWAY telling it like it is

'I do think most fans are realistic. You will always get the grumblers, no matter what happens in life. It just so happens the grumblers make more noise than the rest of the people with common sense.'

GORDON STRACHAN

'Sometimes you want them to still love you and it's not going to happen, but that's life.'

ASHLEY COLE on Arsenal fans

'I hope he stays at Wigan next season, I don't want people to "kill" him.'

Wigan Athletic's MIDO defends team-mate Amr Zaki

'The Leeds fans are going absolutely mad and they have every right to.'

BBC commentator BARRY DAVIES watches referee Ray Tinkler award a blatantly offside goal to West Brom in the 1971 title run

'They pay money to watch Arsenal win. Then when we do not play well, not give our best performances on the pitch, they are very angry. I do not blame them.'

EMMANUEL EBOUE on being booed by the crowd at the Emirates Stadium

'There's my dad, my two brothers and about 20 lads who go everywhere – home and away – and some of the tales they tell are unbelievable. If I'm not involved in football when I finish playing I'll be joining my dad, my brothers and my mates going to watch the games in Europe.'

JAMIE CARRAGHER on his intention to become a fan

'Supporters aren't silly. They not only want skill – they want the passion my players showed today.'

Tottenham Hotspur manager
GERRY FRANCIS

'I can vividly recall my last game for Liverpool. We beat Crystal Palace 9–0 and at the end I threw my boots into the Kop. By the time I left the pitch only my shorts remained on me. The fans were just fantastic.'

JOHN ALDRIDGE

'Well, a lot of fans are sensible about it. He's gone, he's made us a lot of money, let's look forward. But that "Die Rooney" stuff is unacceptable. My little lad was the mascot at the Man United game the other week, and Wayne patted him on the head. My little lad was made up, and up in the stand he asked me, "Why's everyone booing Wayne? I thought you didn't boo good players?"'

ALAN STUBBS on Wayne Rooney's departure for Manchester United

'At a board meeting, he made a big show of how he wanted to make an important point. We all waited expectantly and then he said that we should get rid of Captain Blade. That was it. That was all he wanted to talk about. The team mascot. The fluffy thing on the touchline. Captain F***ing Blade. That was the extent of his contribution.'

Sheffield United manager NEIL WARNOCK on actor Sean Bean

'I was pleased about being booed. Maybe France fans were upset to see a dangerous player. I'm not worried.'

CRISTIANO RONALDO

'I don't care whether people love me or hate me, I'm so pleased I held this club up for four years.'

Peterborough owner BARRY FRY

'I have a lot of respect for Liverpool fans and what I did, the sign of silence – "shut your mouth" – was not for them, it was for the English press.'

JOSE MOURINHO

*'He was brilliant in **Saving Private Ryan**. It would be a real honour if he came and watched us play.'*

MARTIN O'NEILL hams it up for celebrity Aston Villa fan Tom Hanks

'The first game I ever went to was an Aston Villa game and so I am an Aston Villa fan.'

Conservative Party leader DAVID CAMERON

'Give's a kiss.'
BRIAN CLOUGH makes his peace with Nottingham Forest supporters after clipping them round the ear at the end of a match against QPR in 1989

'There is a genuine bunch of fans and then there is a fickle mob who get on your back very quickly.'
Aston Villa manager DAVID O'LEARY hits out at his critics

'Staying away is the last thing any of us wanted to do, but sadly, it was necessary for Albion fans to make the ultimate gesture of any football supporter.'
BRIGHTON FANS' statement explaining the boycott of the home game at Mansfield to protest against the club's board

'I would want an intimidating atmosphere and I count on our supporters to be strongly behind the team in a fair way.'
ARSENE WENGER

'The Kop the night we won the Second Division championship was brilliant. Somehow, I got thrown in there after the game and was mobbed by what seemed like thousands. I must have been in there for 20 minutes.'

Liverpool centre-half RON YEATS

'Sometimes you wonder, do they understand the game of football? Away from home our fans are fantastic, I'd call them the hardcore fans. But at home they have a few drinks and probably the prawn sandwiches, and they don't realize what's going on out on the pitch. I don't think some of the people who come to Old Trafford can spell "football", never mind understand it.'
ROY KEANE

'I'm thick-skinned and they can say what they want about me. I have had it all my life. I just don't want them on the players' backs. The radio phone-ins are terrible. They picked probably the six or seven fans who are disgruntled with me.' Blackburn Rovers manager PAUL INCE

'The crowd was dead. It's the quietest I've heard them here. It was like a funeral.'

SIR ALEX FERGUSON after a home game against Birmingham City

'It is almost like a police state in football now and, if you do stand up, people will take your arm and put it behind the back of your neck and throw you out of the ground.'
COLIN HENRIE, spokesman for the Independent Manchester United Supporters' Association

'There were four or five hundred of our fans there and I swear I bought 1,500 drinks. I spent a fair few quid.'
Plymouth manager IAN HOLLOWAY celebrates an away win in style

'The fans all had the complexion and body scent of a cheese-and-onion crisp and the eyes of pit-bulls.'
Novelist MARTIN AMIS at QPR

'Bill Oddie, Bill Oddie, Rub your beard all over my body!'
READING FANS against Derby

FASHION

'I think the one man representing the essence of a football player is Wayne Rooney. I love his bulldog face and bright red complexion. I would love to design for him and for Rio Ferdinand too – I like his cruel mouth and Ursula Andress hair.' Fashion designer **ANN-SOFIE BACK**

'I used to spend loads of money on Armani. I wouldn't bother going to the shop, I'd just get them to bring the shop to my house.'

DAVID JAMES

'I think a few of the lads will be getting a haircut and getting the fake tan on.'
Ayr United manager BRIAN REID discovers a cup tie against Kilmarnock will be televised

'I moisturize daily with Nivea and I regularly use Nivea body lotion.'
FREDDIE LJUNGBERG

'It's down to 5mm in length. In the past I had braids and cornrows, but I'm done messing around with my hair.'
RIO FERDINAND

'We've got guys from all over the world bringing their style in. The French boys have the tightest trousers. Their jeans are very snug.'
RIO FERDINAND on the Manchester United dressing room

'I get bored quickly and like to change things – except my wife.'
DJIBRIL CISSE on his eclectic taste

'I didn't ignore him but I didn't do what he said either. I just gelled it back to make it look shorter.'
ROBBIE SAVAGE remembers ignoring some pointers on his hairstyle from Sir Alex Ferguson when a youth team player at Manchester United

'I am not gay. But gay men can be very fashionable, so maybe it's a compliment.'
FREDDIE LJUNGBERG on what people have said about him

'Everybody at Arsenal dresses well – they have to. When a player lacks taste in what he wears, he finds his outfit dumped in the dustbin, and we take the mickey out of him.'
SAMIR NASRI

'Beckham is the ultimate fashion victim. His white Stringfellow pants on holiday in the summer were the final straw.'
Eve magazine's ALICE KODELL

'He represents a notion of modern masculinity: as a sports hero, husband and father. He is also a man with a great sense of style. There was a time when soccer players were not always considered to be fashion role models. David Beckham has helped to change that.'
GIORGIO ARMANI

'Footballers are more interested in fashion than before. Not all of them are David Beckham. Some have no idea. But they get photographed all the time and you see them out, shopping with their wives. It wasn't like that in my day.' *GEORGE BEST*

'Stephen Hunt knows my feelings on hairbands – they're banned. It's just jealousy on my part.'
Reading manager STEVE COPPELL

'When I began training with Zenit I had to miss a lot of classes. I transferred to the clothes design department. I have designed several garments myself.'
ANDREI ARSHAVIN

'Ronnie makes a real effort. He looks the part, though that wasn't the case when he arrived. I reckon it's down to my guidance.'
RIO FERDINAND on Cristiano Ronaldo

'I can wear a little bit of heel but when it comes to playing the next day, your feet just kill you. Not anything revealing either – I don't want to look trashy.'
LIANNE SANDERSON of Chelsea's Women's Premier League squad

FOOTBALL WISDOM

'If you've been out for a night and you're looking for a young lady and you pull one, some weeks they're good-looking and some weeks they're not the best. Our performance today would have been not the best-looking bird, but at least we've got her in the taxi.'

IAN HOLLOWAY after QPR's victory against Chesterfield

'Some people believe football is a matter of life and death. I'm very disappointed with that attitude. I can assure you it is much, much more important than that.'

BILL SHANKLY

'All that I know most surely about morality and obligations I owe to football.'
ALBERT CAMUS

'If you want to make a dream happen, it happens.'
GERARD HOULLIER

'Natural ability is far too precious to be messed about with.'
BILL SHANKLY

'It's not about the long ball or the short ball, it's about the right ball.'
BOB PAISLEY

If you have only one passion in life – football – and you pursue it to the exclusion of everything else, it becomes very dangerous. When you stop doing this activity it is as though you are dying. The death of that activity is a death in itself.' ERIC CANTONA

'English players play with their hearts, Europeans with brains. Football played with the heart is more beautiful but not as successful.'
GIANLUCA VIALLI

'One of the biggest things that happened in Creation.'
Sunderland manager ALLAN BROWN on the invention of football

'The missing of chances is one of the mysteries of life.'
SIR ALF RAMSEY

'It's always been a philosophy at this club to keep possession. Make things hard for the opposition.'
SIR ALEX FERGUSON

'If I go to my crazy philosophy I will always say my players are the best in the world and they are the best squad in the world, but that is my crazy philosophy.'
JOSE MOURINHO

'Imagination is your limitation. If someone tells you you can't do that, you should ask, "Why?"'
KEVIN KEEGAN

'If they want to put him on the dark side I have to push him up. If they want to put him on the moon, I have to kick him.'
JOSE MOURINHO on keeping a player's feet on the ground

'If you lose your temper, you lose your brain.'
SVEN-GORAN ERIKSSON

'It is necessary to judge geniuses by their deeds and not by their life.'
JORGE VALDANO

'You don't deliberately fall out with people. It just happens. But once it's over, it's all done and dusted. I don't bear grudges.'
TOMMY DOCHERTY

'Good football and winning trophies are the same thing.'
ARSENE WENGER

'Our love for the game all began when we were children. It's beautiful to be part of the football world.' FRANK RIJKAARD

FOREIGNERS

'In England, they say that Manchester is the city of rain. Its main attraction is considered to be the timetable at the railway station, where trains leave for other, less rainy cities.' NEMANJA VIDIC

'The man who comes to take care of my piranhas told me that if I left West Ham he would kill all my fish.'

PAOLO DI CANIO

'Sometimes I dive, sometimes I stay up.'
DIDIER DROGBA

'Hello, my sharks, welcome to the funeral.'
CLAUDIO RANIERI greets the media shortly before his sacking

'My English might be bad, but I try to make jokes just to keep the spirits up.'
ELANO

'I will never stay to live in England, that's for sure. You get only a brief glimpse of sunlight before it's all cloudy again.'
NEMANJA VIDIC

'My dad throws a good dart. I'm not bad. I will probably hit two or three bullseyes in every ten darts and I nearly threw a 180 once. The first two went in the treble but then I hesitated, thinking, "Oh my god," and the third dropped just below the wire. Damn!' ROBIN VAN PERSIE

'I didn't come here for the culture or the climate, but I want to adapt. I have discovered Newcastle Brown Ale and my ambition is to speak Geordie as well as Peter Beardsley.'

David Ginola

'People looked at me strangely and by the time I found out, it was too late.'
GIANFRANCO ZOLA on being taught English by Dennis Wise

'From 1966 to 1996 there were no foreign players in England and you didn't win any more or less.'
ARSENE WENGER on the fortunes of the England team

'I object to the reaction in England and the use of the term "crazy". Somebody who is crazy gets a gun and kills people in the street. It's not somebody who shoves a referee. You cannot call me crazy for that.'
PAOLO DI CANIO on the reaction after he pushed over referee Paul Alcock

'We really know what the English life is like. We even eat beans on toast.' MIKAEL SILVESTRE

'The dog is fine in Portugal – that big threat is away – you don't have to worry about crime anymore.'
JOSE MOURINHO reassures the authorities after the quarantine row involving his Yorkshire terrier

'In England, they always had more fair play and that's great. But they also had more flaws, more phobias, probably because most English players come from uneducated, lower-class backgrounds. They aren't as conscious of the importance of what they're doing.'
MARCEL DESAILLY

'We won't be bringing our own meat over here. Our bags will be full of football kit. We will eat English food and we will drink English beer.'
JURGEN KLINSMANN on preparations for Euro 96

'When I see all my legs out, I have confidence. I look at my muscles and they look big and I feel strong. With big shorts, I can't see my muscles at all.'
PAOLO DI CANIO

'Of course, there are districts where Roman shouldn't go on his own. The first place that springs to mind is Croydon. It's populated with predominantly low-income folks.'
ALEXEI SMERTIN offers Roman Pavlyuchenko his snapshot of London life

'I will never forget a man crossing the street I met a short time after I got there – he said to me that he worked all week just to think of the pleasure that would be waiting for him at the stadium.' *FERNANDO TORRES*

'I hear how all the English football commentators pronounce my last name – but I can't even reproduce it. It sounds so distorted. I can't even say it.'
ROMAN PAVLYUCHENKO

'People are amazed that I can understand the Scouse accent so well but it is very easy after Glasgow.'
MIKEL ARTETA on his move from Rangers to Everton

'To tell the truth it seemed less difficult on TV. Only now do I understand how dynamic and hard the football is here.'
ANDREI ARSHAVIN

'It has been a mess, a soap opera, and it is very regrettable. I always think private things should be private. When I meet English people going to games and restaurants I like them, but I can never understand this sick interest in private lives.'
SVEN-GORAN ERIKSSON on press intrusion

GREAT RIVALRIES

'People said, "Great! Better, much better, that the goal was so unjust, so cruel, because it hurt the English more."'
CESAR LUIS MENOTTI, former Argentina manager, on Maradona's 'Hand of God' goal

'When an Italian tells me its pasta on the plate I check under the sauce to make sure.'

SIR ALEX FERGUSON on Italian love of a 'smokescreen'

'To score a goal after all the stick I've had from Manchester United fans over the last ten years – well, it's nice to rub it in a bit.'
STEVEN GERRARD

'I hope Chelsea win. I don't like Manchester United.'
JAMIE CARRAGHER previews the 2008 Champions League final

'The important thing was we got the three points.'
Chelsea's WAYNE BRIDGE gets confused after a Carling Cup final win over Arsenal

'The truth is, I envied them for all the success their team was having.'
GARY NEVILLE on Liverpool

'He looks across, sees it's me, sticks his thumbs up, beckons me to wind down my window. So I do, and he winds down his window, leans over with a big friendly grin on his face and says, "Eff off, you red bastard" and drives off.'

PADDY CRERAND on Manchester City fan Bernard Manning

'I used to hate taking corners because they could touch you. A lot of the time nobody wanted to take them.'

NIGEL CLOUGH remembers playing for Nottingham Forest away to Derby

'Everyone thinks they have the prettiest wife at home.'

ARSENE WENGER on Sir Alex Ferguson and his allegiance to United

'We were good friends until we started winning, then he started changing his mind.'

RAFAEL BENITEZ on Jose Mourinho

'I will never answer any questions any more about this man.'

ARSENE WENGER on Sir Alex Ferguson

'To not apologize for the behaviour of the players to another manager is unthinkable. It's a disgrace, but I don't expect Wenger to ever apologize; he's not that type of person.'

SIR ALEX FERGUSON on 'Pizzagate', the post-match food fight involving Manchester United and Arsenal in 2004

'Hopefully the first tackle I'll win the ball and take someone out as well.'

Cardiff City's JOE LEDLEY looks forward to the game against Swansea City

'A friendly encounter.'

GLASGOW PRESS preview of the first encounter between Celtic and Rangers in 1888

'This terrible tragedy must help to curb the bigotry and bitterness of Old Firm matches.'

JOCK STEIN reflects on the Ibrox stadium disaster in 1971

'He became a hero there forever after planting a Galatasaray flag in the middle of the Fenerbahce pitch. They are still selling T-shirts celebrating the moment.'

BRAD FRIEDEL on Graeme Souness

'There are some guys who, when they are at home, have a big telescope to see what happens in other families. He speaks, speaks, speaks about Chelsea.'

JOSE MOURINHO calls Wenger 'a voyeur'

'But I'll tell yer, you can tell him now, he'll be watching it, we're still fighting for this title and he's got to go to Middlesbrough and get something. And I'll tell yer, honestly, I will love it if we beat them... love it.'

Newcastle United manager KEVIN KEEGAN on Sir Alex Ferguson in 1996

'Robbie Savage told me he had bumped into a guy at a petrol station who said, "I don't care if you lose 25–0 at Anfield as long as you beat the Villa." I think that's the attitude of most of our supporters.'
Birmingham City's **PAUL DEVLIN**

'We didn't underestimate them. They were a lot better than we thought.'

BOBBY ROBSON on Cameroon in 1990

'I have played in the Manchester derby, I've played in Arsenal-Spurs and our derby up here is a different derby altogether. It is on a planet of its own.'
NIALL QUINN, Sunderland chairman, on the Tyne-Wear derby

'I always say that if we went to war alongside them, we are entitled to play a football match with them, for God's sake.'
SIR BOBBY CHARLTON laments the end of home internationals between England and Scotland

'It's such a fierce encounter and, God, the matches were intense. Hatred is not too strong a word to use.'
ANDY LEGG, who played for both sides, remembers Cardiff City v Swansea City derbies

GEORGE BEST

'I spent a lot of money on booze, birds and fast cars. The rest I just squandered.'

'In 1969 I gave up women and alcohol – it was the worst 20 minutes of my life.'

'I saw an advert on the side of a London bus inviting me to "Drink Canada Dry".'
On his motivation for joining Vancouver Whitecaps

'I once said Gazza's IQ was less than his shirt number and he asked me: "What's an IQ?"'

'If I'd been born ugly, you'd never have heard of Pele.'

'I think I've found you a genius.'
SCOUTING REPORT on the school-age Best that was sent to Old Trafford

'I wouldn't have been surprised if he hadn't turned up today.'
DENIS LAW joking to fellow mourners at Best's funeral in 2005

'Football has lost one of its greats, and I have lost a dear friend. He was a marvellous person.'
SIR BOBBY CHARLTON

'We had our problems with the wee fella, but I prefer to remember his genius.'
SIR MATT BUSBY

ICONS

ERIC CANTONA

'Anyone who is different or is slightly out of the norm is considered crazy.'

'When the hooligan called me "a French son of a bitch"... I had heard it 50 billion times before. However, on that day I did not react as I used to. Why? I never found any answer to that.'

On his altercation with a fan at Selhurst Park which cost him a nine-month ban in 1995

'Leaving a club is like leaving a woman. When there's nothing left to say, you go.'

Heading out of Leeds in 1992 to join Manchester United

'I did not have the flame any more. Football was my life, my childhood passion. When the flame disappears, why continue? To go to the Middle East for €300 billion? I was not interested in that.'

On his decision to retire

'I do not support France. I am French but I'm not interested in France.'

'This is quite an elitist film and I'm not sure that every Manchester United fan would like it. It's not an action movie that you might go to to relax.'

Reflecting on his role in *L'Outremangeur* (The Overeater) in 2003

'Cantona gave interviews on art, philosophy and politics. A natural room-mate for David Batty, I thought immediately.'

HOWARD WILKINSON on his cultured new signing

JOHAN CRUYFF

'It's better to fail with your own vision rather than following another man's vision.'

'The street taught us. Football is simple. But the hardest thing is to play football in a simple way.'

'I only decided to become a manager when I was told I couldn't.'

'When you saw Cruyff off the pitch he was like a thin boy. But on the pitch he was from another planet.'

RINUS MICHELS, Holland manager

'The great strength of the English game, which worries all foreigners, is its pace, the quick movement of the ball forward. But midfield carries the balance of every match. Control the midfield and you control the game. So long as English teams allow themselves to be outnumbered in midfield they will not exploit their advantages.'

'Of course, winning is important but to enjoy yourself is very important. It's not like the Italians 30 years ago, defending and saying, "We have to win. How? It doesn't matter." It does matter.'

'Why not? It's 11 v 11, the field is the same size. The biggest change is that a lot of people paid attention to the physical side and forgot the technical side.'

On a renaissance for 'Total Football'

DIEGO MARADONA

'I worked hard all my life for this. Those who say I don't deserve anything, that it all came easy, can kiss my a**e.'

'The English are absolutely terrified of us. They are quaking in their boots.'
Before World Cup 2002

'If I had gone to Japan, if I had been with the lads, maybe it could have been different... Seeing Bati crying, the Little Witch Veron, the Little Clown Aimar, Almeyda. Poor lads.'
After the early exit from World Cup 2002 that included a 1–0 defeat by England

'The people voted for me. Now they want me to share the prize with Pele. I'm not going to share the prize with anybody.'
On Fifa's decision to announce joint winners of the Player of the Century

'A little bit the hand of God, a little the head of Diego.'
On his controversial first goal against England in 1986

'Fifa cut off my legs just when I had the chance to prove to my daughters that I could play with 20-year-olds.'
Remembering a failed drug test at World Cup 94 which ended in expulsion

'They are judging me for the 12 years I played in Europe, something Pele did not do. Let's be serious: don't compare me with him any more.'

EDSON ARANTES DO NASCIMENTO PELE

'Success is no accident. It is hard work, perseverance, learning, studying, sacrifice and, most of all, love of what you are doing or learning to do.'

'When football stars disappear, so do the teams, and that is a very curious phenomenon. It is like in the theatre, in a play, where there is a great star. If the star is not well, the whole cast suffers.'

'For 20 years they have asked me the same question, who is the greatest? Pele or Maradona? I reply that all you have to do is look at the facts – how many goals did he score with his right foot or with his head?'

'A penalty is a cowardly way to score.'

'If I was playing today I wouldn't have scored 1,200 goals, I would have scored 2,400 – double the amount – because there is better protection.'

'I scored a lot of goals, a lot people forget; every World Cup they show the save. They don't talk about the goals, they talk about the save.'
On Gordon Banks' save from his header in the Brazil v England match in 1970

'He could shoot with his left, with his right, and he had such vision that as soon as he got the ball he already knew what he was going to do with it. He was extraordinary.'
PAOLO AMARAL, Brazil's fitness trainer

FRANZ BECKENBAUER

'Germany needs to have a handicap, like in golf. They ought to start each match with two goals in advance to their opposition.'

'Some teams take failure and use it as a reason to come back stronger. They build up again and use the memory to their advantage. That is what Germany appear to have done. Other teams use failure as an excuse for more failure and it becomes a mental block.'

'He's a great mate. As a player, he was marked out by intelligence rather than strength. He was more Brazilian than German as a footballer.'
PELE

'The message he sent out was, "Don't even try it. Coming out to face me is a waste of your time."'
SIR BOBBY CHARLTON

'He's a gentleman, a perfect Englishman. Unfortunately, he's not English.'
KEVIN KEEGAN

'A truly impressive person. If you don't like him, there's something wrong with you.'
MICHEL PLATINI

'We played a superb tournament, it was a wonderful final against England, even though my job was to shadow Bobby Charlton. They deserved to win the title, whether or not Geoff Hurst's second goal was a goal.'

On World Cup 66

KENNY DALGLISH

'When I first signed [for Liverpool] in 1977 John Toshack gave me two bits of advice, don't lose your accent and don't over-eat. So at least I got one right.'

'I just made the runs knowing the ball would come to me.'
IAN RUSH on his partnership with Dalglish

'You might as well talk to my six-week-old daughter, you'll get more sense out of her.'
To a reporter interviewing Alex Ferguson after Liverpool v Manchester United

'Of all the players I have played alongside, managed and coached in more than 40 years at Anfield, he is the most talented.'
BOB PAISLEY

'Beautiful teeth, arms wide, that's how he celebrated. He wasn't that big but he had a huge arse.'
BRIAN CLOUGH

'He's the moaningest minnie I've ever known.'
JOHN BOND

'Whatever angle you come in from, you're liable to find his backside in your face.'
DAVID O'LEARY

ICONS

BOBBY MOORE

'There should be a law against him. Bobby knows what is happening 20 minutes before anyone else.' *JOCK STEIN*

'We were all very, very disappointed and upset with ourselves. I think Alf Ramsey showed his true self here when between full-time and extra-time, and before we started extra-time, he gave us all the confidence that was needed when he said that "You've already won the World Cup once, now you've got to go and win it again," and we all thought, how right you are.'

On the World Cup final 1966

'England will win, and that man is the reason why. He can already see in his mind's eye a picture of himself holding up the World Cup, and he's calculated down to the last detail just what that will mean to him.'

West Ham manager RON GREENWOOD on Moore in 1966

'He did not know the meaning of the word panic. He put the rest of the players at ease. He was the best defender, the best reader of play, and a superlative captain.'

ALAN BALL

'I've only ever been associated to West Ham, and I think being in the East End, among the cockney people, has been a great help indeed. They're a very loyal and respectful bunch of supporters at West Ham and a joy to play in front of.'

THIERRY HENRY

'I've never thought of myself as a star. The word disturbs me.'

'Sometimes I get more pleasure at giving a goal, than to score it. My mind is not, "I need to score today." I want to help. If we lose 4–2 and I've scored two great goals, I will still be fuming. Maybe I don't have that selfishness that makes some strikers special.'

'Ketchup here, ketchup there, you put ketchup on everything! Don't you want to taste the food?'
On the English palate

'None of the great goalscorers in history can compare with his assist record. Nobody.'
ARSENE WENGER

'Because of my seniority, the fact that I was captain and my habit of screaming for the ball, they would sometimes give it to me even when I was not in the best position. So in that sense it was good for the team that I moved on.'
On leaving Arsenal

ZINEDINE ZIDANE

'I have a need to play intensely, to fight every match hard.'

'Zidane has an internal vision. His control is precise and discreet. He can make the ball do whatever he wants. But it is his drive which takes him forward. He is 100 per cent football.'
AIME JACQUET, coach of the 1998 World Cup-winning team

'It was inexcusable. I apologize. But I can't regret what I did because it would mean that he was right to say all that.'
On his red card for head-butting Marco Materazzi

'Zidane is my hero and I have always admired him a lot.'
MARCO MATERAZZI

MICHEL PLATINI

'He didn't run a lot like Cruyff and didn't depend on his physique, but I liked how he was the brain organizing things on the pitch.' **PELE**

'When a player is as successful as he was, there's always the risk they'll end up doing something stupid, like Maradona. He, on the other hand, was always calm, quiet and friendly.'
STEFANO TACCONI, team-mate at Juventus

'When I was a kid and played with my friends, I always chose to be Platini.'
ZINEDINE ZIDANE

'Platini was a truly wonderful competitor who was successful everywhere he went. [He] was also a great team leader, a symbol for the rest of his team-mates.'
GERARD HOULLIER

'It should have been our World Cup. That's what football is about. It's tragedy and heartbreak as well as winning. It is also about values – it's about good and evil.'
MICHEL PLATINI on World Cup 1982

FERENC PUSKAS

'You can only kick with one foot at a time. Otherwise you fall on your arse.'

'We didn't know about Puskas. None of these players meant anything to us. They were men from Mars as far as we were concerned.'
BOBBY ROBSON on England v Hungary, 1953

'Of all of us, he was the best. He had a seventh sense for soccer. If there were 1,000 solutions, he would pick the 1,001st.'
Hungary team-mate NANDOR HIDEGKUTI

'The man was a supertalent.'
Real Madrid team-mate ALFREDO DI STEFANO

'He had a roly-poly physique but a wonderful left foot and he was a brilliant finisher.'
SIR TOM FINNEY

LUIZ NAZARIO DA LIMA
RONALDO

'The best player I ever worked with? Tough competition, but it has to be Brazil's Ronaldo.'
SIR BOBBY ROBSON

'To hold the World Cup in my hands, which I have just experienced, is one of the most incredible moments of my life. If I was asked about my wildest dreams, I would never have considered this.'
RONALDO after scoring two goals in the 2002 World Cup final victory over Germany

'We lost the World Cup but I won another cup – my life. I don't remember what happened but I went to sleep and, like the doctor said, it seems I had a fit for about 30 or 40 seconds.'
RONALDO remembers the medical drama ahead of the 1998 World Cup final

CRISTIANO RONALDO

'Skill and courage are very important. If you don't have courage, you can't do the skills.'

'It was paradise watching George Best play, just as it is now with Ronaldo. The difference is that Ronaldo is stronger and faster.'
SIR BOBBY CHARLTON

'When you expect him to be on the left, he turns up on the right. When you expect him to shoot with his left, he shoots with his right.'
LUIZ FELIPE SCOLARI

'It was always said there will never be another to match Best, but I think Ronaldo can become even better than George was.'
PADDY CRERAND

STANLEY MATTHEWS

'He ranks alongside players like Pele, Maradona and Cruyff – and he was one of ours.' SIR BOBBY ROBSON

'Stan was magic. We all like dribblers and he was the wizard. I would study him and think, "What makes him better than anybody else?" My uncles said, "Just watch his first 10 yards."'
SIR BOBBY CHARLTON

'Don't ask me how I do it. It just comes out of me under pressure.'
STANLEY MATTHEWS on his 'swerve'

'Stan would bring the ball squarely to me so that I would never know whether he would go inside or outside. He would lean so far that it was obvious that he had to go that way, but his balance is so perfect he could then sway away and go the other way.'
JOE MERCER on facing the 'swerve'

INJURIES

'The knee still hurts, that isn't going to go away. I have to accept that. Did that tackle end my career? Well, I never played a full game again, did I? It seems like a great coincidence, don't you think?'

ALF-INGE HAALAND on his clash with Roy Keane at Old Trafford

'That's great, tell him he's Pele and get him back on.'

JOHN LAMBIE, Partick Thistle manager, when told a concussed striker no longer knew who he was

'Even in the dressing room afterwards, I had no remorse. My attitude was, f*** him. What goes around comes around. He got his just rewards. He f***ed me over and my attitude is an eye for an eye.'

ROY KEANE on Alf-Inge Haaland

'Robbie had to come off with cramp – in his hair.'

STEVE BRUCE, Birmingham City manager, gets all sarcastic about Robbie Savage

'My only reaction is that it was a freakish incident. If I tried to do it [hit Beckham's face] a hundred times, or a million times, it couldn't happen again. If it did, I'd still be playing.'

SIR ALEX FERGUSON after aiming a kick at a stray football boot in the dressing room which flew off and left David Beckham with a head wound

'It gave me grief.'

ALAN WRIGHT, diminutive Villa full-back, who developed knee strain trying to reach the accelerator of his new Ferrari. He swapped it for a more modest Rover 416

'He is walking a bit like John Wayne at the moment.'

A CLUB INSIDER reveals Sunderland's Kevin Kyle scalded his groin while warming up milk for his eight-month-old son

'The first time that I noticed that something was missing from my hand was when it started to hurt. And it hurt tremendously.'

PAOLO DIOGO, Servette midfielder, who lost the top half of his finger when his wedding ring caught on a fence when he ran into the crowd after scoring a goal. He was booked for excessive celebration

'It's like having a Rolls-Royce in the garage.'

JUANDE RAMOS on Ledley King's recurring knee problems which keep him out of so many games

'When I looked, the leg was lying one way and my ankle was pointing towards Hong Kong, so I knew I was in serious trouble.'

ALAN SMITH, who was injured for Manchester United at Anfield in the FA Cup

'My doctor said to me quite early on that my leg might have to be amputated, then that I might never walk or run again. That didn't help; it was not what I needed to hear.'

Coventry City defender DAVID BUSST after his injury against Manchester United in 1996

'He was watching television and had his foot up on the coffee table. He had it there in a certain position for a number of hours... and strained a tendon behind his knee.' DAVID O'LEARY on Rio Ferdinand's bizarre injury at Leeds United

'If somebody is injured, he should leave the pitch. I would have left if I knew that me neck was broken. I am neither crazy nor stupid.'

BERT TRAUTMANN remembers the 1956 FA Cup Final

'Tony was devastated. He was the first at the hospital the next day. But I wasn't angry, it was a complete accident.'

Arsenal skipper Tony Adams' overzealous celebrations leave goal-scoring hero STEVE MORROW with a broken arm at the League Cup final in 1993

'The dog might have been a small one, but it just happened to be solid.'

CHIC BRODIE, Brentford goalkeeper, whose career came to an end in 1970 when he collided with a sheepdog which had run on to the pitch. The dog got the ball; Brodie shattered his kneecap

'He had no pulse. He looked so pale.'

France's MICHEL PLATINI on the condition of Patrick Battiston after a collision with West Germany's goalkeeper Harald Schumacher during the 1982 World Cup

LEEDS UNITED

'I hated playing against them, I really did. They also had a hell of a lot of skill, too, but they were still a bloody nightmare.' GEORGE BEST *on his battles with Leeds*

'What was called cynical in this country was called professional when the Italians played it.'

BILLY BREMNER

'When you had a girlfriend, he'd have her checked out and make sure she was the right sort of person, in his opinion.'
PETER LORIMER on Don Revie

'There were still times when it made me throw up.'
NORMAN 'BITES YOUR LEGS' HUNTER on the cocktail of sherry and raw egg he was given daily by Don Revie

'He used to talk about taking baths in the sink. It was a poor upbringing and that left him determined that everything went well later on the monetary side.'
ERNEST HECHT, business associate of Don Revie

'When he plays on snow he doesn't leave any footprints.'
DON REVIE on Leeds and Scotland midfielder Eddie Gray

'Me and Billy Bremner had this thing where we'd pass trouble on to each other. So Billy put in a few tackles on Keegan and was giving him a bit of the verbals. He must have hit a raw nerve because suddenly Keegan started punching him.' JOHNNY GILES on the Charity Shield punch-up in 1974

'I know Allan Clarke thought Clough was the best manager he'd worked under. Brian was at his best building clubs up from nothing. He had an ageing team at Leeds that needed changing, but he tried to do it too quickly.'

DUNCAN McKENZIE

'Leeds is a great club and it's been my home for years, even though I live in Middlesbrough.'
JONATHAN WOODGATE

'Lukic saved with his foot, which is all part of the goalkeeper's arm.'
BARRY DAVIES

'That Johnny Giles of Leeds is a great player. Beats me why Alf Ramsey has never picked him for England.'
Scotland manager WILLIE ORMOND on the Irish midfielder

'Winning the league title was a fitting reward for their efforts as well. That team definitely doesn't get the credit it deserves for what they achieved and I think a lot of that is to do with prejudice against Leeds United.'
HOWARD WILKINSON on winning the title in 1992

*'How many love stories do
end well?'*
PETER RIDSDALE

*'As they hit the net I was still
heading his chest. How utterly
good he was, and no edges to him.
He remains that big, amiable
genius who came up from Swansea
to sign for Leeds without even an
overcoat to his name. A centre-half
who never fouled anyone on
purpose in his life.'*
Blackpool's JIMMY ARMFIELD
remembers the power of John Charles

*'Don't be daft, sir, I don't have
a car.'*
JOHN CHARLES remembers his reply
to a Leeds director who offered him
free petrol after scoring a hat–trick

*'What are you doing here? This is
my hero.'*
NELSON MANDELA greets Lucas
Radebe

'To be a
top player,
I think you
need that
edge. Alan
Smith and
David Batty
have got it
here.'
DANNY MILLS

*'Last year destroyed me. Everybody lays the blame on somebody, mainly
on Peter Ridsdale for blindly following a dream, and allowing David
O'Leary to spend too much, but I was no different to any fan. When we
were playing Barcelona and Real Madrid, I wasn't saying, "Don't buy
this or that player, don't spend too much money." I was saying, "Ooh,
go on then. Buy him."'*
NORMAN HUNTER on Leeds' financial problems

LIVERPOOL

'For a player to be good enough to play for Liverpool, he must be prepared to run through a brick wall for me, then come out fighting on the other side.' **BILL SHANKLY**

'I remember Jimmy Adamson crowing after Burnley beat us, that his players were in a different league. At the end of the season they were.'

BOB PAISLEY

'The gaffer sent me to see whether I could spot a weakness, and I found one. The half-time tea is too milky.'
Shrewsbury coach KEVIN SUMMERFIELD recalls a scouting mission to Anfield

'It's there to remind our lads who they're playing for, and to remind the opposition who they're playing against.'
BILL SHANKLY on the 'This is Anfield' sign in the players' tunnel

'Put a sh*t hanging from a stick in the middle of a passionate, crazy stadium, and some people will tell you it's a work of art.'
Real Madrid sporting director JORGE VALDANO shows his appreciation for Liverpool

'Mind you, I've been here during the bad times too – one year we came second.'
BOB PAISLEY

'He's worse than the rain in Manchester. At least the rain in Manchester stops occasionally.'
BILL SHANKLY on Brian Clough

'I hate talking about football. I just do it, you know?'
ROBBIE FOWLER

'He was pretending to graze like a sheep. It's a celebration he picked up from Rigobert Song.'
GERARD HOULLIER explains Robbie Fowler's 'cocaine-sniffing' goal celebration

'Anyone who doesn't learn from Ian Rush needs shooting.'
ROBBIE FOWLER

'Liverpool are magic, Everton are tragic.'
EMLYN HUGHES

'Liverpool without European football is like a banquet without wine.'
ROY EVANS

'Sometimes I feel I'm hardly wanted in this Liverpool team. If I get two or three saves to make, I've had a busy day.' RAY CLEMENCE

'It broke my heart to leave Liverpool.' *KENNY DALGLISH*

'It's best being a striker. If you miss five then score the winner, you're a hero. The goalkeeper can play a blinder, then let one in... and he's a villain.'

IAN RUSH

'Anybody who plays for me should be a bad loser.'
GRAEME SOUNESS

'It's not nice going into the supermarket and the woman at the till is thinking, "Dodgy keeper."'
DAVID JAMES

'Shanks was the father figure, but Roger Hunt was something special. It might sound daft but just picking up his sweaty kit gave me satisfaction.'
PHIL THOMPSON

'We don't have any splits here. The players' country is Liverpool Football Club and their language is football.'
GERARD HOULLIER

'At Liverpool we never accept second best.'
KENNY DALGLISH

'I owe Bob more than I owe anybody else in the game. There will never be another like him.'
KENNY DALGLISH on Bob Paisley

'I go by records and Bob Paisley is the number one manager ever.'
ALAN HANSEN

'Rafa is a magician, a master tactician and a wonderful man. He is a great man, make no mistake about that.'
DAVID MOORES, chairman

'Carra came up to me after extra time and said, "Remember Grobbelaar and the rubbery legs of '84 – and do the same. Dance, do anything, put them off!"'
JERZY DUDEK on Jamie Carragher's advice prior to the Champions League final penalty shootout in Istanbul in 2005

'You can't build a cathedral in a day. A look at the club's history tells you these things take time.'
GERARD HOULLIER

'Bill was so strong it was unbelievable. You couldn't shake him off the ball. It didn't matter where he was playing, though I suppose his best position was outside-left. He could go round you, or past you, or even straight through you sometimes.'
BOB PAISLEY on Billy Liddell

'I just hoped that after the trials and tribulations of my early years in management, someone up high would smile on me and guide my hand. My plea was answered when we got Kenny Dalglish. What a player, what a great professional.' BOB PAISLEY

'Liverpool's fans are just amazing. The best feeling I have at away games is Anfield. It is just incredible. I love it. You get goose bumps when you see their supporters sing "You'll Never Walk Alone".'

THIERRY HENRY

'How could I leave after a night like that? It was the greatest night of my life.'
STEVEN GERRARD reflects on the final in Istanbul

'Amazing, astounding, awe-inspiring, breathtaking, extraordinary, hair-raising, heart-stirring, magnificent, marvellous, miraculous, moving, overwhelming, spectacular, spine-tingling, striking, stunning, stupefying, stupendous, wonderful.'
LIVERPOOL'S OFFICIAL WEBSITE after their Champions League fightback

'We are the real people's club.'
SAMMY LEE responds to Everton manager David Moyes' description of his team

'Who's bigger than Liverpool?'
JAMIE CARRAGHER when asked if he'd thought of moving to a bigger club

LOWER LEAGUE

'I was told the club had debts of £650,000, but it turned out that was just the overdraft. The actual debts were £3.1m. I had to get a loan from Allied Dunbar just to pay the wage bill, and I guaranteed it with my house, my pension, everything. I had to sell everybody, and then we got relegated.'

BARRY FRY sums up his plight as owner of Peterborough United

'I've told the players we need to win so that I can have the cash to buy some new ones.'

**CHRIS TURNER,
Peterborough
manager**

'Dumbarton's Steve McCahill has limped off with a badly cut forehead.'
TOM FERRIE

'And in the other game Bournmouth and Hereford drew 1–0.'
Newsreader MOIRA STEWART

'I'd been ill and hadn't trained for a week. Plus I was out of the side for three weeks before that. So I wasn't sharp. I got cramp before half-time as well. But I'm not one to make excuses.'
CLINTON MORRISON at Birmingham City

'Blimey! The ground looks a bit different to Watford. Where's the dog-track?'
LUTHER BLISSETT on his arrival at the San Siro

'Stan could be the most generous man in the world one minute, but he was pure evil the next. He'd threaten to have you encased in a motorway bridge, things like that.'

BARRY FRY remembers his relationship with Barnet owner, 'ticket tout' Stan Flashman

---

'If Stan could pass a betting shop the way he can pass a ball, he'd have no worries.'

ERNIE TAGG, Crewe manager, on the early days of Stan Bowles

'Gathering everybody back for the first day's training was pretty harrowing. I remember thinking to myself, "Christ Almighty, what have we to do to get out of this league?"'

Wycombe Wanderers manager MARTIN O'NEILL on missing out on promotion to the Football League on goal difference

'We haven't bought a player for five years, and we only spend what we've got. Getting through to this stage is a real bonus, there's a chance of making life a bit easier for everybody.'

Altrincham manager GRAHAM HEATHCOTE on the club's first appearance in the first round proper of the FA Cup in 2007

'There are thousands of kids in the area who'd have their legs chopped off to play for Brighton.'

ROBBIE SAVAGE

'We threw everything at them: the kitchen sink, golf clubs, emptied the garage and threw it at them. Unfortunately, it was not enough, but at least my garage is tidy.'

IAN HOLLOWAY after QPR lost to Watford in the FA Cup quarter-finals

'Graham is the Marje Proops of football. If a player has a problem, Graham will talk it through until the player is right in the head.'

DAVID REYNOLDS, chairman of Kidderminster Harriers, on manager Graham Allner

'I do it as a hobby. I don't drink, I don't smoke, this is how I spend my money.'

Shareholder PETER JORDAN on Woking

'We're still the Dons. Without Wimbledon we wouldn't be here. They had two sons, AFC and us. I'd love to play them one day.'

PETE WINKLEMAN, chairman of MK Dons

'I know some supporters don't like it when I refer to us as a "small club", but a few of them need to take off the blinkers and look at our average attendance.'

JIM HARVEY, manager of Forest Green Rovers

'I'd always thought, "Why don't fans have a say in team selection? We pay the wages." I thought this could be a viable alternative. I look at a lot of lower-league clubs, all of them losing money, and it doesn't make a lot of sense. I was always captivated by the idea of a club that does not have to rely on its local support but has global support, and the internet allows you to do that.'

WILL BROOKS on the philosophy behind the creation of Ebbsfleet United through the website myfootballclub.co.uk

LOYALTY

'I want to let everyone know that I am a Tottenham Hotspur player, I love the club and everyone at the club. I don't always smile so much, but that does not make me a bad person.' *DIMITAR BERBATOV*

'I've been a fan all my life and it'll be fantastic at the end of my career to look back and say I have been with Liverpool all the way through.'
STEVEN GERRARD

'If I played for Milan against United next year I would want to win it, even though I am a United fan.'
DAVID BECKHAM

'Deep down he's still a Blue. It never leaves you. If Wayne could go to Goodison and watch a game without any hassle he'd be the first one there.'
ALAN STUBBS on Wayne Rooney

'Chairmen come and go but as a supporter you will always have a club in your heart.'
GLENN HODDLE on Spurs

'It's been a love affair. I spent the best years of my life here.'
NIALL QUINN on Sunderland

'Milan never has bad blood with anyone and I think that this is the secret and the philosophy that has made the difference over these years.'
PAOLO MALDINI

'You don't want to be a b******. It's not a good thing to show disloyalty sometimes.'
KENWYNE JONES at Sunderland

'I think that if you go to another team, especially from another country, it's difficult to gauge the enormity of what it means to lose to Man United. Those lads won't know what it means to the fans every day at work. They will be upset because they have personal pride, but they don't know what it means, like I know what it means.'
Fulham's DANNY MURPHY, Liverpool fan and ex-player, on the importance of having a nucleus of local talent

'To return to Lazio would be a beautiful madness. It's like an ended love – it was ten years ago and now the curiosity is to see if it can start again.'
PAOLO DI CANIO

'The T-shirt incident is a massive regret in my career. But although we'd won promotion, I had already told Peter Reid, the manager, that I was thinking of moving. In hindsight, joining Sunderland was a mistake. A mistake because of my background. Everyone knows I'm Newcastle through and through.'
LEE CLARK reflects on being photographed wearing a T-shirt bearing the legend 'Sad Mackem bastards' while on the books at Sunderland

MANAGERS

'[He] detested shabby appearance, unkempt hair. I always insisted that my players looked smart. He wouldn't stand any nonsense on the field, no arguing with the referee. Nor would I... Most of all he taught me that a football club manager is boss.' BRIAN CLOUGH on his manager at Sunderland, Alan Brown

'It was a game of two halves, and we were rubbish in both of them.'

**BRIAN HORTON,
Oxford United manager**

'Our training methods are equal to anybody's. We've got fitness and conditioning specialists, a dietician – even paedo-bloody-philes, or whatever you call them.'
ROY EVANS expresses his pride in the Liverpool backroom staff

'I would have given my right arm to be a pianist.'
SIR BOBBY ROBSON

'I am getting a new kitchen put in, so there is no way I'll let them sack me until I get full use out of it!'
GORDON STRACHAN reponds to rumours he will be sacked

'We can't replace Gary Speed. Where do you get an experienced player like him with a left foot and a head?'
SIR BOBBY ROBSON

'I'm very pleased for Paul, but it's like watching your mother-in-law drive off a cliff in your new car.'

TERRY VENABLES as Paul Gascoigne sets off for Lazio

'You must be as strong in March, when the fish are down.'

GIANLUCA VIALLI

'When you are 4–0 up you should never lose 7–1.'
LAWRIE McMENEMY

'The way forwards is backwards.'
DAVE SEXTON

'The important thing is he shook hands with us over the phone.'
ALAN BALL

'Hartson's got more previous than Jack the Ripper.'
HARRY REDKNAPP

'My own autobiography, which was written by Ian Ross...'
HOWARD KENDALL

'He's such an honest person it's untrue.'
BRIAN LITTLE

'The 33 or 34-year-olds will be 36 or 37 by the time the next World Cup comes around, if they're not careful.'
KEVIN KEEGAN

'There is great harmonium in the dressing room.'
SIR ALF RAMSEY

'Coaches nowadays produce clones of themselves: cautious players with a negative attitude.'
KEVIN KEEGAN

'Every player who comes here is under scrutiny from the moment he arrives. I know the colour of their eyes, every one of them.'
BILL SHANKLY

'Managing a football club is a draining job, it drains your body and your brain.'
DON HOWE

'When managers win matches, people talk about how they changed players; if they don't win, then it becomes "rotation policies".'
RAFAEL BENITEZ

'There was a photo of him in one of the local papers the other day showing him pushing against a goalpost and the wind had got under his magnificent head of hair and lifted it three or four inches. He looked like one of those mad professors. When you start getting to 50, never mind 67, the stress in present-day managing is so fierce.'
BRIAN CLOUGH on Sir Bobby Robson

MANCHESTER CITY

'I can't see any downside to this to be honest. Going from a cult football club that black cab drivers in London all like and patronize you [about], to being the richest club in the world is just staggering. I always kind of knew that 40 years of loyalty would be repaid somehow and I always knew that a day would come when we stagger everyone in football. It'll be nice to know that every gallon of petrol a Manchester United fan buys is going into our transfer kitty.'

Musician NOEL GALLAGHER on the takeover of the club by the Abu Dhabi United Group in 2008

'The thing about City is they possess the most loyal fans in the world. They laugh and sing and joke and carry inflatable bananas when things are going badly and they do exactly the same when things are going well.'

STUART HALL

'We've got a history of not building on good situations. We could have jumped into the European shake-up, again we couldn't make that leap.'

KEVIN KEEGAN

'If I wasn't praying for City, just think where we might be.'

MCFC chaplain TONY PORTER

'If you want my personal opinion they bottled it.'

Executive chairman GARY COOK on the failure to reach agreement with AC Milan for the £100 million transfer of Kaka to Eastlands

'One of my mates heard before me. He rang me to say, "We've signed Robinho." I just went, "Yeah, whatever…" I mean, he's the sort of player you would usually only pick for City in a computer game.'
MICAH RICHARDS

'To concede a penalty and have Richard Dunne sent off was a bad start, but we were in the game until it was 3–0.'
SVEN-GORAN ERIKSSON on City's 8–1 drubbing by Middlesbrough

'We really have deep pockets.'
DR SULAIMAN AL-FAHIM, Abu Dhabi United Group

'If you don't try to reach the stars you will not even reach the top of the trees.'
SVEN-GORAN ERIKSSON on Thaksin Shinawatra's ambition to make City 'the next United'

'Tell the fans from me that they cannot love the club more than me. We have the same goals and they will understand me now. Mark Hughes, Garry Cook, Jo, maybe Ronaldinho. They will see by the new season.'
THAKSIN SHINAWATRA

'Maybe there are certain people who want to see me fail, but it's predictable we will be criticized if we lose games. People say we should be doing better because we are the richest club in the world, but it's not fair to judge us like Liverpool, Arsenal, Chelsea or Manchester United.'
MARK HUGHES

'I don't want those scally City fans round at my house putting my windows in when City are in the Third Division and blaming it all on me.'

NOEL GALLAGHER responds to suggestions he should become chairman

'I have seen it all before and I think a lot of people are over-reacting. Franny Lee was such an expert at it that he used to trip himself up.'

TONY BOOK
on the controversy surrounding Premiership players diving

'Watching Manchester City is probably the best laxative you can take.'

PHIL NEAL

'We were supposed to come out at half-time to do a draw at Maine Road once, but Frank Clark said, "I don't want those two tossers on the pitch," and we respected him for that.'

MARK and LARD

'That was when the boys grew up. They laid a bogey in their mind.'

JOE MERCER on a 3–1 defeat of United on the way to the title in 1968

'It has to be the second goal I scored during the last-ever Maine Road derby. I heard the fans singing a new song: "Who let the Goat out?" and I thought, "I'm having that one!"'

SHAUN GOATER on his favourite strike

MANCHESTER UNITED

'They've done us proud. They came back with all their hearts to show everyone what Manchester United are made of. This is the most wonderful thing that has happened in my life and I am the proudest man in England tonight.'

MATT BUSBY following United's 4–1 victory over Benfica in the European Cup final in 1968

'Has any chairman since Mao had more faith in his own opinions than Ken Bates? If laying down the law was an Olympic sport the Chelsea chief would be staggering under the weight of gold medals.'

SIR ALEX FERGUSON

'Rooney can do the lot. He will eventually have all the United goalscoring records. I don't even see why he can't overtake my 46 in a season.'
DENIS LAW

'People used to say that if I'd shot John Lennon, he'd still be alive today.'
GARRY BIRTLES on his goalless run with United

'Becks hasn't changed since I've known him. He's always been a flash Cockney git.'
RYAN GIGGS

'It is necessary to wear the sandals of humility and not let the win over Manchester United go to our heads.'
Vasco Da Gama coach ANTONIO LOPES

'Paul Ince and I sat in the directors' box with Alex Ferguson and he said, "There's a kid playing tonight who's going to be special." Ryan was still at school. I think he was 15, and we saw this spindly little pipe cleaner of a footballer running amok on the left-hand side. You could see straight off that he had a special gift.'

GARY PALLISTER recalls his first sight of Ryan Giggs

'For me I love Manchester United. Yes for sure I would like to go home or to Spain at some stage, but right now I am very happy here.'

CRISTIANO RONALDO

'Manchester United 0, Heaven 1. This will be one of the great signings.'

SUPPORTERS hang a banner at Old Trafford commemorating the death of Sir Matt Busby

'Poborsky's had one or two moments – two, actually.'

DES LYNAM

'Manchester United are breathing down the heels of Liverpool now.'

GARY NEWBON

'It is a hard one to take because I thought we were the better team and the score does not reflect that.'

SIR ALEX FERGUSON is obstinate about Manchester United 1, Liverpool 4

'Fergie said I was a Manchester United player in the wrong shirt – I said he was an Arsenal manager in the wrong blazer.'
TONY ADAMS

'And now for international soccer special: Manchester United versus Southampton.'
DAVID COLEMAN

'If you want me to rule out ever being Manchester United manager, I can't. Special clubs need special managers, so in theory it could work.'
JOSE MOURINHO

'I always had a reputation for going missing – Miss England, Miss United Kingdom, Miss World...'
GEORGE BEST

'There have been a few players described as the new George Best over the years, but this is the first time it's been a compliment to me.'
GEORGE BEST on Cristiano Ronaldo

'United get the rough end of the stick from the media so it's only natural that I stand up for them. When Eric Cantona kicked that idiot at Crystal Palace, I was interviewed on the radio and a woman from Belfast comes on and says that was the worst thing she had ever seen. I said, "You live in Belfast and you're telling me that you haven't seen anything worse?"'
PADDY CRERAND

'There are times when you want to wring his neck. He hangs on to the ball when players have found better positions. Then out of the blue he wins you the match, and you know you're in the presence of someone special.'

PADDY CRERAND on George Best

'I was pretty upset, to be honest, because I had so many friends at United. I was just relieved not to get any real stick. And that turned out to be my last touch in domestic football.'

DENIS LAW, then playing for Manchester City, remembers the audacious back-heel that condemned United to relegation in 1974

'It seems impossible to hurt him. All manner of men have tried to intimidate him. Best merely glides along, riding tackles and brushing giants aside like leaves.'

JOE MERCER, Manchester City manager

'Rooney has signed a deal to do five books. That's an awful lot of crayons.'

DJ JOHNNIE WALKER

*'F*** off, I've got a pub to run and goats to feed.'*

Thinking it is Ally McCoist taking the mickey, ANDY GORAM fields Sir Alex Ferguson's phone call asking him to join United

'Where are you going? You've got a game tonight.'

SIR MATT BUSBY tells a limping Denis Law he can forget taking the day off

'He had this mop of blond hair which stood up in the wind. I bet he wishes he had it now.'

BILL FOULKES remembers his first sight of Bobby Charlton in 1953

'Any manager in the world would like a player like Giggs in their side, and I am no different.'

Brazil coach CARLOS DUNGA

'People have underestimated Sheringham. But Teddy's come up trumps again.'

Pundit TERRY VENABLES praises the scorer of United's equalizer in the Nou Camp

'We beat United in the League Cup final and, afterwards, Alex put his hand out and said, "Well done, big man." It made me wish I had gone up to him first.'

PAUL McGRATH on beating United with Aston Villa

'Normally when you swap shirts they are soaked in sweat, but Beckham's smelt only of perfume. Either he protects himself against BO or he sweats cologne.'

Inter's RONALDO

'We were all such friends... I couldn't understand how I could have been 50 yards away from the aeroplane, still strapped in my seat, without suffering anything but a bang on my head. How could that be? How could I feel myself all over and find out that I was all right, completely whole, and my pals were dead?... I think about this every day of my life.'

BOBBY CHARLTON on the Munich disaster

'From now on we have three major trophies to win, and like I told the boys in the dressing room, "You have already won the Champions League and Premier League." The only one who hasn't is me. I really want to win those trophies so I can say to the other players, "I am one of you."' DIMITAR BERBATOV

'I think it was Jock Stein who told me there's nothing wrong with losing your temper for the right reasons – and I think 70 to 80 per cent of the time I've done it for the right reasons.'

SIR ALEX FERGUSON on giving his players 'the hairdryer treatment'

'I want nights like this again.'
RYAN GIGGS in Moscow, 2008, when he made his 759th appearance for the club, breaking the record held by Sir Bobby Charlton

'Humility, feet on the ground, never changed. It's amazing that you can come through a whole career like that.'
SIR ALEX FERGUSON praises his fellow knight, Sir Bobby Charlton

'A tabloid offered me £50,000 to slag him off, and others have, but I wouldn't. I have too much respect for the guy.'
NORMAN WHITESIDE on Sir Alex Ferguson

'I'm the only manager ever to be sacked for falling in love.'
TOMMY DOCHERTY

MIDDLESBROUGH

'I drive to York, to Whitby, to Robin Hood's Bay. Beautiful places to go if you have a day off to enjoy with your family. For me and my family, it's perfect here.'
EMMANUEL POGATETZ countering any negative perceptions of the Middlesbrough area

'I have spoken with a lot of fans over the last few weeks and they ask me about Gareth Southgate. But the magic wand in our situation isn't sacking Gareth Southgate.'
STEVE GIBSON on the relegation battle

'If I had to fly to the moon I'd take Tony Mowbray, my captain, with me. He's a magnificent man.'
BRUCE RIOCH

'I can't see how one kebab can be the difference between beating one or three men or running from box to box or scoring a goal. Bloody hell, in Scotland I had haggis and won the double.'
PAUL GASCOIGNE on his kebab break with Danny Baker and Chris Evans

'I would certainly bring in Juninho, Ravanelli and Emerson again. But maybe I should have brought in two or three top-drawer players, rather than five average ones.'
BRYAN ROBSON on doing things differently

'We called him vampire because he didn't like crosses.'
STUART BOAM on goalkeeper Jim Platt

'I'll never forget the support they gave me and everything they did for me. In England, life was so totally different, calmer in some ways, quiet but pleasant. I have a good feeling about everything in England, except that one game, against Leeds.' **JUNINHO**

'I was under pressure up at Middlesbrough, even though people were saying I was in a no-lose situation. I thought, "Oh yes, are you mad? It's my name which is on the team if they go down. That's what they will label you with. Terry Venables – the man who took Middlesbrough down."'

TERRY VENABLES

'The Northern Echo? *You'll be after a Middlesbrough line. It's time to get my depressed face on then.'*

GARY PALLISTER attempts to lighten the mood in the face of press enquiries about the relegation battle

'I'll have to put up the barricades.'

DARREN WILLIAMS scores the winner for Sunderland against his home-town club

'After each game I would come in with my nose wrapped around my head while he looked immaculate and went out for the night in the same clothes he had arrived in. And he kept collecting the man-of-the-match award. I thought there was something not quite right here, but it worked.'

STUART BOAM on Willie Maddren

MOMENTS OF MADNESS

'I've been to the Vatican and seen the gold ceilings. And then I hear the Pope saying that the Church was concerned about poor kids. So? Sell the ceilings, mate! You've got nothing going for you. You were only a goalkeeper.' DIEGO MARADONA

'I worked in a sausage factory. My brother took me for the interview on his motorbike, but I couldn't get the crash helmet off. I had to do the interview with the visor up. I got the job, but when I turned up a week later to start, the boss didn't recognize me. He thought I was delivering something.'

CHRIS WADDLE

'They were all crazy in there. One said he was Napoleon and they didn't believe him. I said I was Maradona and they didn't believe me either!'

DIEGO MARADONA on his spell in a psychiatric hospital

'They say every dog has his day. And today is Woof Day. I want to go out and bark.'

QPR manager IAN HOLLOWAY celebrates the club's promotion in 2004

'Me.'

ZLATAN IBRAHIMOVIC in answer to the question: who is your role model and idol?

'Even Jesus Christ only had one Pontius Pilate – I had a whole team of them.'
KEN BATES after standing down from the Wembley National Stadium Board

'Communism v Alcoholism.'
SCOTTISH BANNER at a Soviet Union v Scotland game

'I've got an old one, about 53 years old. Not very big. We have a little bit of land in Cornwall. It's a different world down there. Single-track lanes, a bit like Greece. It's always tomorrow.'
NEIL WARNOCK reveals he is the proud owner of a tractor

'They would drink so much that they could not stand up. Where I came from no player would do that.'
SLAVEN BILIC on the perils of going out for the night with English team-mates

'I can't stand ankle socks. When a man crosses his legs and the trouser leg rides up to show hairy shins, it offends my eyes.'
FABIO CAPELLO

'I feed anything. I feed foxes. I'm not supposed to but I love it. The squirrels get a lot – I bought the plastic containers, they chewed the bottom and the nuts fell out so I had to buy the steel ones. They work better.' HARRY REDKNAPP

'If you wanted a new pair of shoes you went down the swimming baths in bare feet and just nicked a pair.'

TOMMY DOCHERTY on his early life

'Sometimes it can be a project to go for a walk in this country. You have to think about an umbrella, a coat, and before you've packed you're tired.'

PETER SCHMEICHEL on life in Britain

'Oh no, I dare not risk the wrath of that lass from the Gorbals.'

SIR ALEX FERGUSON on how his wife can be just as intimidating as he is

'I met him in Japan because he was over there, although he did not stay for very long because he didn't like the sushi.'

ARSENE WENGER on Luiz Felipe Scolari

'They shot the wrong bloody Kennedy.'

BOB PAISLEY is less than impressed with the performance of Alan Kennedy

'He used to have extra butter on his, too. My nan used to see his spindly legs. She thought he needed feeding up. My roll didn't.'

JAMIE REDKNAPP on the cheese rolls his grandparents supplied to him and team-mate Steve McManaman

'I like the Lindisfarne version, but Gazza's was rubbish. He gave me a signed copy of it, but I think I melted it down on the bonfire.'
CHRIS WADDLE on 'Fog On The Tyne'

'I like the nice clothes, the taste in colour. My medallion is made of diamonds and it has the names of my mum, my wife and my daughter on it. Everything on me is diamond, but it all goes in my locker. We have good security and I trust my team-mates.'
EL-HADJ DIOUF

'When he took me down to Fulham I lived with him for five months in his flat near Harrods. I did the cooking, actually.'
PETER BEARDSLEY on Kevin Keegan

'I lost control for a few seconds.'
CRAIG BELLAMY on confronting team-mate John-Arne Riise with a golf club

'I started looking through it and I thought, "They've missed out his pages, where are the lines?"'
VINNIE JONES on discovering his character in the film *Gone in 60 Seconds* is a mute

'The man who lived here before was a fox hunter. But when I moved in, the hunt had to ask for my permission to use the land. Unluckily for them, I hate hunting and I said, "Look somewhere else." I don't care what they thought about me – I'm an animal lover.'
DJIBRIL CISSE

MOURINHO

'I'm not a defender of old or new football managers. I believe in good ones and bad ones, those that achieve success and those that don't. Please don't call me arrogant, but I'm European champion and I think I'm a special one.'

'If I wanted to have an easy job... I would have stayed at Porto – beautiful blue chair, the Uefa Champions League trophy, God, and after God, me.'

'Sometimes you see beautiful people with no brains. Sometimes you have ugly people who are intelligent, like scientists. Our pitch is a bit like that. From the top it's a disgrace, but the ball rolls at normal speed.'

'When I saw Rijkaard entering the referee's dressing room I couldn't believe it. When Drogba was sent off I didn't get surprised.'

'If you ask me if I jump with happiness when I know Mr Poll is our referee? No.'

'Many great managers have never won the Champions League – a big example is not far from us.'
On Arsene Wenger

'How do you say "cheating" in Catalan? Barcelona is a cultural city with many great theatres and this boy has learned very well. He's learned play acting.'

On Lionel Messi

'As we say in Portugal, they brought the bus and they left the bus in front of the goal. I would have been frustrated if I had been a supporter who paid £50 to watch this game because Spurs came to defend. There was only one team looking to win, they only came not to concede – it's not fair for the football we played.'

'I don't regret it. The only thing I have to understand is I'm in England, so maybe even when I think I am not wrong, I have to adapt to your country and I have to respect that.'

On putting a finger to his lips during the 2005 Carling Cup final against Liverpool

'We have top players and, sorry if I'm arrogant, we have a top manager.'

'The style of how we play is very important. But it is omelettes and eggs. No eggs – no omelettes! It depends on the quality of the eggs. In the supermarket you have class one, two or class three eggs and some are more expensive than others and some give you better omelettes. So when the class one eggs are in Waitrose and you cannot go there, you have a problem.'

'I felt the power of Anfield, it was magnificent. You should ask the linesman why he gave a goal. Because, to give a goal, the ball must be 100 per cent in and he must be 100 per cent sure that the ball is in. It was a goal that came from the moon – from the Anfield stands.'

On the validity of Liverpool forward Luis Garcia's goal in the Champions League semi-final in 2005

'My history as a manager cannot be compared with Frank Rijkaard's history. He has zero trophies and I have a lot of them.'

'Ronaldo is a good player but he is certainly not the best. He deserved the Golden Ball award because his team won the Champions League and the Premier League. But, for me, Ibrahimovic is the best.'

'It's like having a blanket that is too small for the bed. You pull the blanket up to keep your chest warm and your feet stick out. I cannot buy a bigger blanket because the supermarket is closed. But the blanket is made of cashmere.'

On financial constraints

'Places like this [Bramall Lane] are the soul of English football. The crowd is magnificent, saying, "F*** off Mourinho" and so on.'

'If they made a film of my life, I think they should get George Clooney to play me. He is a fantastic actor and my wife thinks he would be ideal.'

'I always wanted to coach a big club in Italy. The job at Inter is a big challenge for me. And I do believe it could be very entertaining for the journalists.'

'If Roman Abramovich helped me out in training we would be bottom of the league, and if I had to work in his world of big business, we would be bankrupt.'

'In five years I have never had a match where my team has had less possession than the opponents.'

'The moral of the story is not to listen to those who tell you not to play the violin but stick to the tambourine.'

'I would love to gather all the fans together to say goodbye, but they would crush me with their love.'

'I am more scared of the bird flu than football. What is football compared with life?'

'I was nine or ten years old and my father was sacked on Christmas Day. He was a manager, the results had not been good, he lost a game on December 22 or 23. On Christmas Day, the telephone rang and he was sacked in the middle of our lunch.'

NEWCASTLE UNITED

'We were driving back from Birmingham when Kieron Dyer suddenly shouted, "Stop the bus! I've left my diamond earring in the dressing room." Can you imagine in my playing days a player telling Bill Shankly, "Stop the bus, Bill, I've left me earring in the dressing room."' SIR BOBBY ROBSON

'Even the ref shook my hand. He could have given me a penalty – that would have been even better.'

ALAN SHEARER after breaking Jackie Milburn's scoring record

'Will I be sitting down with the owner tonight? I don't think it will be tonight. The owner will be going down the town to have a few.'
KEVIN KEEGAN on Mike Ashley

'With all the movement we've got up front, we need someone to stand still... and Mark's that man.'
KEVIN KEEGAN on Mark Viduka

'He's the only player who, when he's on the TV, Daleks hide behind the sofa.'
NICK HANCOCK on Peter Beardsley

144

'My father had five sons. I had four brothers.'
SIR BOBBY ROBSON

'He used to remind me of a wave breaking. He would just surge past defenders with his incredible pace. Everybody loved watching him.'
SIR BOBBY CHARLTON shares his memories of Jackie Milburn in his pomp

'He's started off on the wrong foot and kept on going on the wrong foot. It's hopped along on the wrong foot for about three years now and I think it's time to say goodbye, I really do.'
MALCOLM MACDONALD on Michael Owen

'You always say something good about players who leave. Robert is leaving. Good.'
FREDDY SHEPHERD on the unlamented departure of Laurent Robert

'Kevin Keegan once described me at Newcastle as a monster who needed to be fed. David Ginola and Keith Gillespie on the wings, and Peter Beardsley behind me used to do the feeding.'
LES FERDINAND

'People asked two completely separate questions. One, when I used to go and watch Newcastle. Then someone asked me who was the greatest-ever footballer so I said Jackie Milburn. The two elided together. What a lot of trouble I had over it.'
TONY BLAIR clears up the confusion over whether or not he said he saw Jackie Milburn play as was reported in the press

'The crowd were expecting Craig Bellamy to come on and turn it around in an instant. They think he's a magician. He's not, he will be, but he hasn't got a magic wand. He hasn't played for seven months. He will be an October player. He's not a September player.' *SIR BOBBY ROBSON*

'Hitler didn't tell us when he was going to send over those doodlebugs, did he?'
SIR BOBBY ROBSON explains his reluctance to name his team

'Daft as a brush.'
SIR BOBBY ROBSON on Gazza

'My last game for Newcastle was skippering them in the FA Cup Final, and my next game was as captain of Sunderland – imagine that.'
BOB MONCUR remembers crossing the Tyne-Wear divide in 1974

'Show 'em your backside, Tommy.'
Manager GEORGE MARTIN's advice to winger Tommy Walker

'I'm now a dad who can't take his kids to a football game because I am advised that we would be assaulted.'
MIKE ASHLEY, Newcastle owner

'Ruud wanted our supporters to love him more than Alan.'
ROB LEE on Gullit and Alan Shearer

'I've seen a lot of changes, managers and players. It's alarming if you were to make a list.'

WARREN BARTON on the revolving door at St James' Park

'Somewhere else? Oh yes, maybe, but there's a smell of the northeast which drew me back. I've got black and white blood and I'll stick at it because this is the team I love.'

SIR BOBBY ROBSON

'Whether it's the right time or wrong time, it doesn't make any difference. Alan Shearer's blood is black and white and he'll be telling the players that as well.'

PAUL GASCOIGNE on the appointment of Alan Shearer as manager

'When I read Bellamy for Newcastle, I thought I would have to have another drink, so I had several.'

ALAN SHEARER on the prospects of the Welsh international returning to Tyneside

'You want me out. That is what I am now trying to do… You don't need to demonstrate against me again because I have got the message.'

MIKE ASHLEY to Newcastle fans

'He would go down the pit white and would come up black. There was no colliery bath back then and he would wash in the tin tub we had at home, trying to go from black to white again, but a miner never felt he had entirely cleansed himself of the grit and dust. Then on Saturday he would love to take us to St James' Park because he adored Newcastle United.'

SIR BOBBY ROBSON remembers his father

NOTTINGHAM FOREST

'When I sit in the garden and close my eyes I can still see that moment in Munich when Robertson made his move. Peter Taylor stiffened beside me and grabbed my arm. Robertson is not far from the corner flag. There are half a dozen Malmo players in the box. Trevor Francis is hurtling towards the far post, and Robbo sends over the perfect cross. One – nil. Pass me the European Cup. Thank you.'

BRIAN CLOUGH remembers the winner in the 1979 final

'Just give the ball to John Robertson – he's a better player than you.'

BRIAN CLOUGH advises Trevor Francis ahead of his Forest debut in 1979

'I've just been upstairs to give my chairman [Fred Reacher] a vote of confidence.'

BRIAN CLOUGH

'Punching above the club's weight for 18 years.'

FRANK CLARK on the Clough era

'One of the secrets of [Forest's] success was that everybody underestimated us.'

BRIAN CLOUGH

'He stayed the night. In the morning he just started again. I gave in. He had his breakfast, I signed and he dried the dishes.'
ARCHIE GEMMILL on Clough's determination to sign him for Forest

'We are sometimes presented as a rag-tag and bob-tail bunch, but that is nonsense. John Robertson was a genius, Peter Shilton was the best goalkeeper in the business, Kenny Burns was voted England's player of the year, and Archie Gemmill, Martin O'Neill and Tony Woodcock were all international regulars.'
JOHN McGOVERN on Forest's European Cup winners

'We gave Hamburg a lesson in application, determination and pride – the things we take for granted in English football.'
BRIAN CLOUGH on the qualities that secured his second European Cup

'We were the only team that got fined if we didn't go out for a drink on a Friday evening.'
GARRY BIRTLES

'Together, Peter and Brian were unbeatable, the perfect partnership. Individually, the light of brilliance did not shine from them quite so dazzlingly. Brian's great trick was making the game simple for players, and supplying them with the confidence and self-belief he possessed to a Muhammad Ali-like degree.'
JOHN McGOVERN on the Clough/Taylor partnership

'The night before the 1979 League Cup final we were absolutely blotto. We went to bed at midnight, drunk. I crawled up the stairs on all fours.'

GARRY BIRTLES remembers the build-up to Forest's defeat of Southampton

'It wasn't a great game, but they were a boring team, Malmo. In fact, the Swedes are quite a boring nation. But we still won, so who cares?'

BRIAN CLOUGH

'Shilton wins you matches.'
PETER TAYLOR on why he paid £270,000 for Peter Shilton in 1977

'He was absolutely sensational and I don't think Brian would disagree with us either.'
MARTIN O'NEILL remembers Brian Clough

'We all took stick. It didn't matter who you were, whether you cost £1m or came on a free transfer.'
TREVOR FRANCIS on Brian Clough

'I'm not equipped to manage successfully without Peter Taylor. I am the shop window and he is the goods.'
BRIAN CLOUGH on his partnership with Taylor

'We just gelled together, we filled in the gaps... My strength was buying and selecting the right player, then Brian's man management would shape the player.'
PETER TAYLOR on Clough

'Stan is the player who had the lot and threw it all away. Nobody has ever got inside his head and maybe never will.'
FRANK CLARK on
Stan Collymore

'I went to Chelsea the season after it all happened with Forest, got some stick but scored our equalizer and I knew Baddiel was in the stands so that was a great day. I milked it for all it was worth.'
JASON LEE on the stick he took over his 'pineapple' hairstyle from Frank Skinner and David Baddiel

'There were good times and bad times. I can remember turning up for training and hating his guts, then by the end of training loving the man.'

STUART PEARCE on Clough

'We went out to start the game, you looked at the Forest end and it was chock-a-block, but the Liverpool end was not full. That was a surprise. A few thought it was a bit strange that it was not full and then all of a sudden people were climbing over and you knew something was wrong. This was not crowd violence or anything, something very wrong was taking place.'
NEIL WEBB recalls the Hillsborough disaster

THE OLD DAYS

'We are tempted to wonder whether Association football players will eventually rival thoroughbred yearling racehorses in the market.'

NEWSPAPER REPORT on the £1,000 transfer of Alf Common from Sunderland to Middlesbrough in 1905

'He was the greatest centre-forward I ever saw. But he had more tricks than a bucketful of monkeys.'

FRANK SWIFT on Hughie Gallacher

'Football was my only love, for it is a noble and manly game.'

BILLY MEREDITH

'They keep my knees warm.'

ALEX JAMES on the oversized shorts he wore while playing for Preston North End

'Are you going to grab the headlines again this year, Jackie?'

SIR WINSTON CHURCHILL is presented to Newcastle United's Jackie Milburn before the 1952 FA Cup Final

'Football meant so much to them, you see. It was all they had.'

RAICH CARTER remembers the financial sacrifices made by Sunderland fans to watch their team in the depression-hit 1930s

'I've been V-bombed in Brussels before the Rhine crossing, bombed and "rocketed" in London, I've been in a shipwreck, a train crash, and inches short of a plane accident. But the worst moment of my life, and one I would not willingly go through again, was giving the Nazi salute in Berlin.'

EDDIE HAPGOOD on England's 1938 match against Germany

'Wilf played football the way Fred Astaire danced.'

Brian Clough on
WILF MANNION

'It was typical. There we were going off to a strange country about which we knew very little and there wasn't anyone we could turn to if we were sick or injured. Backward wasn't the word for it.'

EDDIE BAILY on the England squad travelling to World Cup 1950 in Brazil without a team doctor

'I'm glad I'm pretty even-tempered, or I'd have gone across the table at him.'

EDDIE HAPGOOD remembers being goaded by Italy's Pietro Serantoni

'There was something special about the place on those dark, rainy nights. What was extraordinary was the attitude of the fans to foreign sides. There was a tremendous naivety about it all, almost a feeling that these were men from the moon.'

BRYON BUTLER recalls the Molineux crowd's reaction to continental opponents in the 1950s

PORTSMOUTH

'The fans, the players. It's been a difficult year off the field so this is a dream come true. We're a very close family – it's for all my grandchildren and everybody. The players are all great, I love them all.' HARRY REDKNAPP on winning the FA Cup in 2008

'This is the best moment of my life. I started the game and I won the cup for Portsmouth. I have felt nothing like this.'
KANU

'He's cocky and arrogant, but show him a goal and he's away like a wind-up toy.'
HARRY REDKNAPP on Jermain Defoe

'I sorted out the formation last night lying in bed with the wife. When your husband's as ugly as me, you'd only want to talk football.'
HARRY REDKNAPP

'He's the future king of England and I've just done a dance for him – I think it's a bit surreal.'
PETER CROUCH performs the robo dance in front of Prince William

'This is the next step for me. It's like Christmas. It's the best job in the world. I'm scared to bits, of course.'
TONY ADAMS becomes manager

'He was like he is now, gangly. It takes a bit of time but once you see through that initial view, even at that age he was more than just a big boy who headed it.'
PAUL HART on Peter Crouch

'Had I not become a footballer, I think I would have been a virgin.'
PETER CROUCH on *Soccer AM*

PUNDITS

'I never liked pundits before I became one.' ALAN HANSEN

'You win nothing with kids.'
ALAN HANSEN dismisses the title
credentials of eventual champions
Manchester United

*'It looked easier to score, but
Senderos just glanced the ball off
his balding palette.'*
DAVID PLEAT

*'Most players would give their
right arm for Jason Wilcox's
left foot.'*
MARK LAWRENSON

*'Strangely, in slow motion replay,
the ball seemed to hang in the air
for even longer.'*
DAVID ACFIELD

*'Great striking partnerships come
in pairs.'*
NIGEL SPACKMAN

'It's a case of him losing les marbles.'
GARY LINEKER on Eric Cantona

*'Germany benefited from a last-gasp
hand-job on the line.'*
DAVID PLEAT at World Cup 2002

*'It was the game that put the Everton
ship back on the road.'*
ALAN GREEN

*'If it doesn't go right tonight,
Wenger has another leg up
his sleeve.'*
GLENN HODDLE

'Aston Villa are playing the best out
there, West Ham the second best.'
DEAN SAUNDERS

'There are already millions of camera angles showing everything, and referees even have things in their ears now. Pretty soon they'll be going out on to the pitch with a satellite dish stuck up their a**es.' IAN WRIGHT

'He'll take some pleasure from that, Brian Carey. He and Steve Bull have been having it off all afternoon.'
RON ATKINSON

'You could have driven a Midnight Express through that Turkish defence.'
TERRY VENABLES

'Romania are more Portuguese than German.'
BARRY VENISON

'Cristiano Ronaldo has been compared to George Best. The incomparable George Best.'
DAVID PLEAT

'Jean Tigana has spent the entire first half inside Liam Brady's shorts.'
JIMMY MAGEE

'Too many players looked like fish on trees.'
PAUL MERSON hammers England

'Alan Shearer has banged it through a gap that wasn't even there.'
PAUL WALSH

'Jamie Carragher there, looks like he has cramp in both groins.'
ANDY TOWNSEND, Liverpool v AC Milan, Istanbul

'They're wearing the white of Real Madrid, and that's like a red rag to a bull.'
DAVID PLEAT on Chelsea's kit against Barcelona

'You would think that if anybody could put up a decent wall it would be China.'
TERRY VENABLES, World Cup 2002

'The lad throws it further than I go on holiday.' *RON ATKINSON*

'Hagi has got a left foot like Brian Lara's bat.'
DON HOWE eulogizes Romania's Gheorghe Hagi

'Hagi could open a tin of beans with his left foot.'
RAY CLEMENCE is also a fan

'He's chanced his arm with his left foot.'
TREVOR BROOKING

'It was one of those goals that's invariably a goal.'
DENIS LAW

'If you're going to get in behind Rio Ferdinand you've got to show him what you've got and then go in hard.'
JAMIE REDKNAPP

'There's no way that Ryan Giggs is another George Best: he's another Ryan Giggs.'
DENIS LAW

'Wimbledon are putting balls into the blender.'
RODNEY MARSH

'It's like a toaster, the ref's shirt pocket. Every time there's a tackle, up pops a yellow card.'
KEVIN KEEGAN

'Ya beauty. What a hit, son. What a hit.'
ANDY GRAY admires Steven Gerrard's goal

'He's got a knock on his shin there, just above the knee.'
FRANK STAPLETON

'He's good at that, David Beckham. He's good at kicking the ball.'
JIMMY ARMFIELD

'Someone should be hung. Whoever is responsible should be hung and shot at dawn in the morning. I'll do the shooting.'
CRAIG JOHNSTON laments the state of English youth development

'Evra's literally left him for dead there.'

JAMIE REDKNAPP

'Joaquin scuffed that shot with his chocolate leg.'

MICK McCARTHY berates the Spain forward

'And Hyypia rises like a giraffe to head the ball clear.'

GEORGE HAMILTON

'Hakan Yakin plays with Young Boys of Berne.'

JONATHAN PEARCE

'The tide is very much in our court now.'

KEVIN KEEGAN

'It really is an amazing result, nil-nil at half time.'

CHRIS KAMARA

'Arsenal's touch and movement are amazing. I hope the listeners are watching this.'

CHRIS WADDLE

'Lord Nelson, Lord Beaverbrook, Sir Winston Churchill, Sir Anthony Eden, Clement Attlee, Henry Cooper, Lady Diana – we have beaten them all. Maggie Thatcher can you hear me? We have beaten England in the World Cup… your boys took a hell of a beating.'

BJORGE LILLELIEN celebrates Norway's win in a World Cup qualifier in 1981 at the Ullevaal stadium, Oslo

RANGERS

'We've had a lot of situations where people say that Rangers play anti-football, rubbish football or whatever. But, for a first-year team, we've settled in well and, for those teams that have lost to us, if they are that good, why have they not beaten us?' WALTER SMITH

'Managing Rangers or Celtic is extremely stressful, worse than Liverpool.'

GRAEME SOUNESS

'He's got a groin strain and he's been playing with it.'
ALEX McLEISH

'He was a magician on the park. He could have put a size-five football in an egg cup.'
SIR ALEX FERGUSON on Jim Baxter

'Celtic manager Davie Hay still has a fresh pair of legs up his sleeve.'
JOHN GREIG

'I'm an East Kilbride boy. I couldn't even spell lawyer in those days, far less have one. No, I represented myself. Mind you, I did appeal a three-match ban and after speaking at the hearing it was increased to five.'
ALLY McCOIST

'You lads line up alphabetically by height.'
ARCHIE KNOX

'We were watching **The Bill** *– What was the score in Seville?'*
RANGERS CHANT after Celtic's Uefa Cup final defeat

'We're like chalk and cheese, but we're great friends. You never know, maybe one day the mad duo will be a managerial partnership. It would be chaos. The Christmas party would last a month.'
IAN DURRANT on Ally McCoist

'That was a great player. A left-sided genius for Glasgow Rangers. He was such a great player – truly gifted.'
RUUD GULLIT on Davie Cooper

'Before he came I remember standing on the Tube platform at Ibrox and bumping into one of our players who was eating a sausage supper. He'd just had his pasta lunch at Ibrox. Far from being embarrassed, he offered me a chip.'
Club secretary CAMPBELL OGILVIE remembers life before Graeme Souness

*'In my first game against Rangers at Easter Road, I was a cocky youngster. Willy Woodburn – the ferocious tackler and Rangers and Scotland centre-half in the early 1950s – yelled after I had gone past him with the ball, "George, get that little b*****d!" At the first moment, after the ball had next gone out of play, Young put his massive paw on my shoulder and said gently, "Never mind, son, what Woodburn says – I'll deal with you in my own way," which I knew was fair play.'*
WILLY ORMOND on George Young

'One man arrived and everything was different. Suddenly the historic flow of talent out of Scotland was reversed.'

CAMPBELL OGILVIE, club secretary, remembers the Souness revolution

'Everything I did on the pitch was off-the-cuff. Sheer instinct. If I'd been a good boy maybe the swashbuckling stuff would have got stifled.'

JIM BAXTER

'Lots of people offered me advice but I loved the booze. It's as simple as that, I just loved getting boozed up.'
JIM BAXTER

'He thinks what he wants – I am the boss.'
PAUL LE GUEN on his differences with Barry Ferguson

'It was when Barry Ferguson revealed he had just written his last will and testament and its chief stipulation was that he be cremated in a Rangers shirt that you feared for Paul Le Guen's future as Rangers' manager.'
Columnist DION FANNING after Rangers choose Ferguson over Le Guen

'My relationship with Graeme was all right – until he sacked me.'
GRAHAM ROBERTS on Graeme Souness

'He had a great left foot. As my dad used to say, he could open a tin of peas with that left foot.'

ALEX McLEISH remembers Davie Cooper

'There has to be a limit to anybody's patience. Understanding only goes so far.'

WALTER SMITH after a reckless challenge by Paul Gascoigne

'We want to be champions every time – if we won it ten times in a row it would never get boring.'

JORG ALBERTZ

'I didn't dare say, "No". I would have felt as if I were playing truant from school.'

DICK ADVOCAAT on the persuasive powers of David Murray

'In his prime he was one of the best players in the world. He glided with the ball in a way that made him virtually untouchable for opponents and he was a match-winner.'

BRIAN LAUDRUP on Paul Gascoigne

'Tom Cowan broke his leg and John Brown's Achilles tendon snapped during the game. I always remember John lying on the ground waiting for the stretcher and Mark Walters came over and said to the doctor, "Does he really have to go? I'm feeling my hamstring a bit." If John could have stood up he'd have knocked Mark out.'

ALLY McCOIST remembers Rangers v Aberdeen in 1991

REFEREES

'During the Respect campaign Ferguson was charged by the FA with improper conduct following remarks made against Martin Atkinson and Keith Hackett. He was not punished. He is the only manager in the English league who cannot be punished for these things.' *RAFAEL BENITEZ*

'A lot of tears were shed and it will always live with me. My last thought, before I die, will probably be: why?'

GRAHAM POLL on giving Croatian Josep Simunic three yellow cards during the 2006 World Cup

'I didn't know it was against the rules.'
Brazilian defender CLEBERSON on being booked for kissing the referee

'He has got about as much personality as a bag of chips.'
Wigan manager STEVE BRUCE is less than impressed by Jeff Winter

'He's being smuggled out of our country – this is a disgrace.'
GRAHAM POLL supports Norwegian ref Tom Henning Ovrebo, who received death threats after turning down strong penalty appeals by the home side in the Champions League semi-final between Chelsea and Barcelona

'You cannot assault a referee. He stands between the game and chaos.'
TONY BANKS after Paolo di Canio had pushed over Paul Alcock

'I do swear a lot, but the advantage is that, having played abroad, I can choose a different language from the referee's.'
JURGEN KLINSMANN

'Why can't the fourth official, who is wired up to the referee, have a monitor by the side of the pitch and tell the ref what really happened?'
HARRY REDKNAPP

'To receive a bite was the worst thing that has happened to me since I came to England. The strangest thing was that the referee did not send him off.'
JAVIER MASCHERANO on some overfamiliarity from Jermain Defoe

'You only have to fart in the box to concede a penalty these days.'
Leeds United manager KEVIN BLACKWELL

'Next thing we'll be giving our handbags to the linesmen as we skip on to the field.'
MIKE SUMMERBEE on referees' determination to cut out 'physical' play

'If you see an unruly child you don't blame the child you blame the parent. In this instance the FA are the governing body, the custodians of the game, and it's their job to make sure their children behave themselves.' GRAHAM POLL

'He must be a nightmare to play against because you're never sure what he's going to do next. For that reason he's not always the easiest of players to referee.'
HOWARD WEBB on Wayne Rooney

'I never comment on referees and I'm not going to break the habit of a lifetime for that prat.'
RON ATKINSON

'Whether that was a penalty or not, the referee thought otherwise.'
JOHN MOTSON

'Then he came over, pushed my head down and kneed me in the jaw.'
69-year-old referee ERIC MANN, assaulted for sending off a player in the Manchester Sunday League

'We are getting PC decisions about promoting ladies. It does not matter if they are ladies, men or Alsatian dogs. If they are not good enough to run the line they should not get the job.'
GORDON STRACHAN takes out his frustration on assistant referee Wendy Toms

'Because our standing is gradually being eroded, why should they have respect for us? Because they can say whatever they want about us with no comeback.'
GRAHAM POLL on managers

SCANDALS & CONTROVERSY

'What I do know is that it was not paid to me – not in fivers, not in plastic carrier bags, not in a layby or a motorway service station. Not in any shape or form, not at all.' BRIAN CLOUGH *on allegations he took bungs*

'I made the stupidest mistake ever of my personal life. Anyone can make a mistake, and I made a big mistake.'

Former Brazilian international RONALDO discovers three prostitutes he invited to a motel room are transvestites

'Without the scandals we couldn't have done this.'

GENNARO GATTUSO reflects on the domestic corruption allegations that preceded Italy's triumphant World Cup 2006 campaign

'I was on £50,000 a week until the police found my printing machine.'

Ex-Manchester United winger MICKEY THOMAS, who went down for 18 months for producing his own £10 notes, which he distributed via junior players at Wrexham

'The local girls are far uglier than the ones in Belgrade. Our women are far prettier and they don't drink as much beer.'

GEORGI HRISTOV ruins his chances of pulling during a spell with Barnsley

'You and I have been physically given two hands and two legs and half-decent brains. Some people have not been born like that for a reason. The karma is working from another lifetime. I have nothing to hide about that.'

GLENN HODDLE, who was sacked as England manager for expressing 'personal views'

'There was no mistaking it was Wayne Rooney because he was dead ugly.'

Call girl CHARLOTTE GLOVER alleges Wayne Rooney was one of her customers

'After he'd filled the dishwasher he led me up the stairs to his bedroom.'

FARIA ALAM on her affair with Sven-Goran Eriksson

'If you don't get out of here we're going to start shooting real bullets.'

DIEGO MARADONA aims an air rifle at reporters

'I am a channel for the Christ spirit. The title was given to me very recently by the Godhead.'

DAVID ICKE, former Coventry City and Hereford United goalkeeper

'I know the Spurs fans have lost people in the war, but I also lost people in the war.'

MARK BOSNICH apologizes for making a Nazi salute at White Hart Lane

'We all make mistakes in life and I am very disappointed to have let Rangers, Scotland, my family, all the fans down.'
ALLAN McGREGOR after he and Barry Ferguson are banned for life from representing Scotland after a late-night drinking session and making v-signs at the camera during a Scotland World Cup qualifier

'A doctor gave it to me for back pain.'
AL-SAADI GADDAFI, son of Colonel Gaddafi, after testing positive for nandrolone. Following a three-month ban he made his Serie A debut for Perugia against Juventus

'I know a lot of people don't think that I deserve another chance and rightly so, but fortunately I have got one.'
JOEY BARTON after leaving prison following a conviction for assault

'For Tony to admit he is an alcoholic took an awful lot of bottle.'

IAN WRIGHT on Tony Adams

'Both Douglas Hall and Freddy Shepherd sincerely apologize for any offence that has been caused to members of their families, the fans of Newcastle, the people of the North East and their fellow directors. They particularly apologize to the women of the North East.'
NEWCASTLE DIRECTORS in a joint statement following a story in a Sunday tabloid in which they allegedly called Newcastle's female supporters 'dogs' and nicknamed Alan Shearer 'the Mary Poppins of football'

SHANKLY

'My idea was to build Liverpool into a bastion of invincibility. Napoleon had that idea and he conquered the bloody world! And that's what I wanted. For Liverpool to be untouchable. My idea was to build Liverpool up and up and up until eventually everyone would have to submit and give in.'

'If a player is not interfering with play or seeking to gain an advantage, then he should be.'

On the offside rule

'It's not your leg... it's Liverpool's leg.'
To Tommy Smith when he complained of an injury

'Chairman Mao has never seen a greater show of red strength.'
On the Liverpool fans

'If you can't make decisions in life, you're a bloody menace. You'd be better becoming an MP.'

'He couldn't play anyway. I only wanted him for the reserve team.'
Downplaying the potential of Lou Macari after the Scottish international opted to join Manchester United

'It's great grass at Anfield, professional grass.'

'Hold on a minute, John Wayne hasn't arrived yet.'

Lightening the mood at the press conference ahead of announcing his resignation

'Laddie, I never drop players. I only make changes.'

'With him in defence, we could play Arthur Askey in goal.'

On centre-half Ron Yeats

'If you are first you are first. If you are second you are nothing.'

'Of course I didn't take my wife to see Rochdale as an anniversary present, it was her birthday. Would I have got married in the football season? Anyway, it was Rochdale reserves.'

'I'm just one of the people who stands on the Kop. They think the same as I do, and I think the same as they do. It's a kind of marriage of people who like each other.'

'If he isn't named Footballer of the Year, football should be stopped and the men who picked any other player should be sent to the Kremlin.' On Tommy Smith

'A lot of football success is in the mind. You must believe that you are the best and then make sure that you are. In my time at Liverpool we always said we had the best two teams in Merseyside: Liverpool and Liverpool reserves.'

'If Everton were playing at the bottom of the garden, I'd pull the curtains.'

'The trouble with referees is that they know the rules, but they don't know the game.'

'You could be right. Mind you, Tom's 57.'

On being told Tony Currie was comparable with Tom Finney

'The end of the season.'

On his worst moment in football

'No, humiliate the bastards.'

When asked whether the team should ease off when 4–0 up at half-time to West Ham

'Just tell them I totally disagree with whatever they're saying.'

To an interpreter at an Italian airport press call

'I've ended a 73-year wait by this club to win this trophy and this is all you think it's worth.'

On being offered a derisory bonus after Liverpool won the FA Cup for the first time

'Football's an inborn thing. Nobody makes players except mothers and fathers. Not coaches.'

'He was a ghost of a player, but grisly and strong. He could have played all day in his overcoat.'

On Tom Finney

'Sometimes my humour aggravates people because I catch them so quickly. When they open their mouths I can shut them up right away with something funny. But I should use my humour and so should everyone else who has it because it brightens up the world.'

'You've got nothing to beat today. I've watched the West Ham players come in. That Bobby Moore can hardly walk, and as for Geoff Hurst... he looks ill to me. Don't be cruel to them. Stop when you've got five.'

Team talk before a West Ham game

'Scotland has a fanfare of trumpets before their last match at Hampden prior to leaving for Argentina. They did all their shouting before they'd kicked a ball. Scottish people have a habit of doing that. And I'm Scottish to the core.'

On Scotland's farewell party prior to the World Cup in 1978

SOUTHAMPTON

'Once you get into debt, the bank manager comes into the club to run the team.' RUPERT LOWE *on football finances*

'Between the semi and the final, Bobby had missed so many it was a standing joke, but, when McCalliog played it through, he found a bottom corner.'

LAWRIE McMENEMY remembers Bobby Stokes goal that won the FA Cup in 1976

'You tell me if there is anyone else in football by the name of Rupert.'

GRAEME SOUNESS on Rupert Lowe

'Alan started life as a road sweeper and ended up as the best lead violinist Southampton ever had.'

LAWRIE McMENEMY remembers Alan Ball

'It was a good save. I just wish he had retired last week.'

GORDON STRACHAN laments a David Seaman save in the 2003 FA Cup Final

'"Finally," Ted was saying, "this year, please try to come into training without alcohol on your breath. Now over to you, Lawrie." And they're all just lazing around, eyeing me up. "Thanks, Ted," I said, "and I liked the joke at the end." But it hadn't got a laugh and later I found out why – he'd been deadly serious. They took a long time to accept me. It wasn't just that Ted had been in charge for 18 years – so had Terry Paine.'

LAWRIE McMENEMY remembers taking over the reins from Ted Bates

STOKE CITY

'We are not at Crufts, we are at Battersea Dogs' Home. We go looking for strays, get them in and cuddle them.' TONY PULIS

'I've got to get Dan Shittu ready for the Stoke game. I've told him to go to Iceland and ask if he can sit in one of their freezers.'

Ian Holloway at QPR, perhaps imagining that Stoke is much further north

'That save from Pele's header was the best I ever made. I didn't have any idea how famous it would become – to start with, I didn't even realize I'd made it at all.'
GORDON BANKS

'The key to combatting Stoke's dangerous long throws and set-piece deliveries is not to crowd the penalty area. It's better to have a clearer area and someone to head the ball... We went man to man and said, "We'll win the ball."'
ROB GREEN

'His name is symbolic of the beauty of the game, his fame timeless and international, his sportsmanship and modesty universally acclaimed. A magical player, of the people, for the people.'
DEDICATION on Stanley Matthews' statue at the Britannia Stadium

'It was in the middle of the night, the dog lies on the stairs and I didn't see him. I trod on him, realized what I'd done, tried to go to the next step, gone over on my ankle and fallen down the stairs.'

LIAM LAWRENCE confirms he will miss the trip to Portsmouth after tripping over his pet Labrador

'If we treat the last 12 games any differently than we have the first 34, we will end up with our pants pulled down and our backsides slapped.'

TONY PULIS

'Even the ballboys are 6ft 4ins here [at Stoke] and we had to stand up to it.'

KEVIN BLACKWELL

'The problem with foreign players is they go down and stay down.'

TONY PULIS tells *The Sentinel*

'It's not a trade secret, people have seen it on TV. They will have watched videos, but if it's done right there is no way of defending it. It doesn't matter what team you are up against, it's going to work if I hit the right areas.'

RORY DELAP on his throw-in

'Once the prayer mats have been left in the dressing room, it'll be a case of defending in numbers, stubbornness, organization, discipline and a lot of luck.'

RICARDO FULLER describes Stoke's preparations ahead of a Man United fixture. United won 5–0

SUNDERLAND

'I knew instinctively the only place Peter [Lorimer] could hit it was to a gap to my left and I knew I had to get up. I jerked my body up and thrust an arm upward in a reflex action, like a man trying to ward off a blow, and pushed the ball on to the crossbar. As I hit the ground again, I turned and saw Malone hooking the ball away. I was back in business.'

JIM MONTGOMERY remembers his spectacular double save against Leeds United in the 1973 FA Cup Final

'I ask myself every day if I'm the right man for Sunderland. I asked myself this morning and I said I was. Sunday morning, if the answer's no, we'll have to look at it.'

ROY KEANE on the pressures of management

'Thanks for giving me the most beautiful moment of my career.'

BOB STOKOE to Jim Montgomery, Wembley 1973

'Nothing I have ever heard equalled that wild Roker Roar.'

DANNY BLANCHFLOWER

'This represents a major coup for our football club.'

NIALL QUINN welcomes Roy Keane

'We were living in Gosforth at the time, when one night there was a knock at the door. My wife, Marj, went to answer it and discovered a funny little man with his collar turned up and his trilby pulled down over his face. The guy didn't say who he was, just that he wanted to speak to me. When I went to see for myself he introduced himself as Jack Hall, team scout for Sunderland. He continued, "I've got Bill Murray, the Sunderland manager, in his car just around the corner and he wants to speak to you."'

LEN SHACKLETON remembers his first contact with Sunderland in 1948

'After we clashed during the Sunderland v United game, I mouthed to him, "Put it all in your next book." He responded by catching me on the side of the head with his elbow. Or, as the Man United fans like to put it, my head hit his elbow.'

JASON McATEER on his clash with Roy Keane

'I am no miracle worker.'
BOB STOKOE in his first programme notes

'The day I walked into Sunderland, putting a smile on the faces of well-paid players was the last thing anybody wanted me to do. Players had been taking the p**s out of the club for years. If they wanted them smiling all the time they should have employed Roy Chubby Brown.'
ROY KEANE

'Sunderland were silly to sell me and Derby were lucky to get me.'
RAICH CARTER leaves his home town club in 1945

'A sporting cathedral in a city searching for international excellence.'

Chairman BOB MURRAY on the Stadium of Light

'We've had years of Newcastle fans calling our ground Joker Park. Now we've handed it to them on a plate. I'm sure they won't take long to come up with something which rhymes with light.'

CALLER to Radio Newcastle phone-in show

'I think I'd have had a struggle to convince people to come and celebrate my career, but this helped, no doubt, by giving it away.'

NIALL QUINN on his announcement that he will give away all the money earned from his testimonial to charity

'I fled from the howling of an approaching black cat, convinced by the influence of the full moon and a warming dram or two that it was the devil incarnate.'

The first mention of a significant local black cat by JOSHUA DUNN, a member of what became 'The Black Cat Battery' during the Napoleonic wars. The position of the black cat in Sunderland folklore was cemented when a black kitten sat in twelve-year-old Billy Morris's pocket at Wembley during the 1937 FA Cup Final as Sunderland beat Preston 3–1.

'It happened in the first half, and at half-time I went straight to the treatment table to see how Cloughie was. Johnny Watters, our physio, just got hold of the bottom half of his leg, from the knee downwards, and the whole lot came forward. That meant his cruciate ligaments were completely gone. I can remember Johnny whispering to me, "That's it."'

Skipper CHARLIE HURLEY remembers the injury that ended Brian Clough's playing career, Boxing Day, 1962

TOTTENHAM HOTSPUR

'The great fallacy is that the game is first and last about winning. It's nothing of the kind. The game is about glory. It's about doing things in style, with a flourish, about going out and beating the other lot, not waiting for them to die of boredom.' **DANNY BLANCHFLOWER**

'We like a tackle at Tottenham. We're not pansies, you know.'

DAVID PLEAT

'Spurs have got to be the best in the land, not the second best.'
BILL NICHOLSON

'We're good enough to survive in the Premiership and maybe have a good cup run, or even earn a Uefa Cup spot if things go really well. But we are never going to win the championship.'
TIM SHERWOOD

'There's only one word for Tottenham's under-achievement – mismanagement.'
DAVID PLEAT

'I haven't just signed a player. I've rescued a lad from Hell.'

BRIAN CLOUGH buys back Steve Hodge from Spurs in 1988

'I don't think Spurs would ever sign a superstar like Klinsmann or Bergkamp again. Those guys are floaters. They'll go anywhere, play for anyone who pays them the most.'

ALAN SUGAR

'I want a consistent team, not a flash one.'

GEORGE GRAHAM

'We looked bright all week in training, but the problem with football is that Saturday always comes along.'

KEITH BURKINSHAW

'Darren Anderton has had so many X-rays that he got radiation sickness.'

ALAN SUGAR

'To be honest we were looking to go to France, Spain or Italy, but Keith [Burkinshaw] was the first to make us an offer. Ricky always says we were lucky to play for Spurs, but they were lucky to have us. The changes since then have been unbelievable. Culturally this country used to be so insular. When we arrived in 1978, we wondered how we would be received. Now look around you at the number of foreigners playing here. Look at the change in attitude towards black players. Viv Anderson was the first England player in 1978 and he was booed by some of the fans. Now there are no problems at all, not in England anyway.'

OSSIE ARDILES on the deal that brought him and Ricky Villa to Spurs in 1978

'I called George in to talk about it at lunchtime. He was defiant and aggressive. He used inappropriate words during the course of the conversation.'

Spurs executive vice-chairman DAVID BUCHLER reveals the behind the scenes turmoil that resulted in the dismissal of George Graham as manager in 2001

'When I joined Spurs, people told me I was their typical player because I had flair. That image was Spurs' strength, their marque de fabrique across the world, but it has been lost along the way. They need to recreate it.'

DAVID GINOLA

'I did really well to hold myself back. I really don't think he realizes how strong I am, otherwise he wouldn't approach me with headbutts and everything.'

MARTIN JOL after a run-in with Arsenal manager Arsene Wenger

'I feel like the guy who shot Bambi. I am not an egotistic loony.'

ALAN SUGAR, Spurs chairman, after sacking Terry Venables

'It sent a shiver down my back.'

JURGEN KLINSMANN on the welcome from Spurs fans on his return to White Hart Lane in 1998

'The worst thing for us was losing Berbatov at the last moment and we didn't have time to sign a new player. But business is business. It was impossible.'

JUANDE RAMOS

'There used to be a football club over there.'
KEITH BURKINSHAW takes a parting shot

'The day I got married, Teddy Sheringham asked for a transfer. I spent my honeymoon in a hotel room with a fax machine trying to sign a replacement.'
GERRY FRANCIS

'Man in the raincoat's blue & white army.'
SPURS FANS avoid chanting George Graham's name

'Our central defenders, Doherty and Anthony Gardner, were fantastic and I told them that when they go to bed tonight they should think of each other.'
DAVID PLEAT

'I won't be making a nuisance of myself. You won't see me hanging round the car park with a dog-end in my mouth.'

TERRY VENABLES on his departure

'It is the man without the ball who is the most important. I can remember an old schoolmaster who tried to show me the way. His words stuck and they always apply: "When not in possession, get into position." I never forgot that phrase. You should never be just watching. I used to say, when one of my players erred in this way, "If I catch you doing that again, I'll charge you admission. If you want to watch, then you should pay."'

BILL NICHOLSON

'Even now, when I go over to my mother's house and dig out the old tracksuit tops I wore, it makes the hair stand up on the back of my neck. I like to think I am part of a special family. I am no longer connected with the club on a daily basis, but I'm delighted with every win and sad about every defeat.' STEVE PERRYMAN on Spurs

'Any skeletons in the closet? Apart from that record with Chris Waddle?'

FA chief executive GRAHAM KELLY interviews Glenn Hoddle for the England job

'I've had so many cards it feels like Christmas.'
EDGAR DAVIDS on a flurry of yellows

'When you've finished playing football, young man, which is going to be very soon, I feel, you'll make a very good security guard.'
DAVID PLEAT to 17-year-old Neil Ruddock

'Ah well, ma'am, you see we all know each other!'
DANNY BLANCHFLOWER to the Duchess of Kent when she asked why the Leicester City players had names on their tracksuits and the Spurs team didn't

'You don't put diesel in a Ferrari.'
HARRY REDKNAPP imposing a booze ban on his players at Spurs after Ledley King had disgraced himself at a Soho nightclub

WAGES

'When I was a kid I used to go the pictures on a Saturday morning and they often showed films of the Klondike gold rush, everybody going crazy and shooting each other, staking out claims. Football is at that stage now, at its barmiest. I am sick of reading more about the money in football than the football.' BRIAN CLOUGH

'Poverty is good for nothing, except perhaps for football.'

Real Madrid's sporting manager **JORGE VALDANO**

'I hope today's players realize how lucky they are. I was quite happy with my three-bed semi and a Ford Escort.'
ANDY GRAY

'I'm a rich guy. I earn £80,000 a week – you earn £10 an hour. I've got nothing to lose, I'm a big star. You, you're nothing in your £10-an-hour job.'
The words a drunken LEDLEY KING is alleged to have used to the doorman when refused entry to the Punk club in Soho

'I had everything. A lovely wife. Lovely kids. Big house. Cars. Great wages. I played for the best club in the country, by far. The fans liked me. And I done that.'
PAUL MERSON on what he threw away

'I signed for Liverpool for £2, ten shillings a week, and I thought, "Blimey, I've made it."'

CHARLIE ASHCROFT remembers his move to Anfield in 1946

'I recently bought an original Dolce & Gabbana suit. It's white with images of tigers on it. It's really bright and out of the ordinary. I wore it to training, and there was a real fuss. Jonathan Woodgate put on my trousers and started jumping around the dressing room, asking, "Do I look like a clown?"'

ROMAN PAVLYUCHENKO on how he likes to spend his money

'They used to say it was eight pounds during the season and six pounds in the summer. They used to drop your wages in the summer as you weren't playing and it didn't matter whether you had contracts or not. Ah, the good old days.'

SIR BOBBY CHARLTON

'If football retains any decency in these days of raging commercialism and gamesmanship, it is only because the game so often acts as a morality play against the dangers of hubris.'

JONATHAN WILSON

'The money to pay the players has to come from somewhere and, inevitably, that means it will come from the pockets of the supporters. I don't believe we should be continually asking the fans to pay higher prices. It makes it impossible to take the family, so you are losing out on the next generation of supporters.'

SIR ALEX FERGUSON

'One night he rang up and said that he had tickets for a Sinatra show so I went to watch it with my wife. The following week I went to pick up my wages and he said that I wasn't going to receive any wages for three weeks – that was to pay for the Sinatra tickets.'

BARRY FRY remembers Barnet chairman Stan Flashman

'Some of the higher wages flying around make the public averse to these bigwig superstars, but at our level they're down-to-earth, honest boys trying to make a living.'
Plymouth Argyle manager IAN HOLLOWAY

'Wages are unbelievable now. You can go to Austria and find people on £40,000 per week.'
GORDON STRACHAN

'He said, "No, netto. I always talk netto."'
Chelsea managing director COLIN HUTCHINSON reveals Ruud Gullit's approach to negotiating a new contract

'I think in football there is too much modern slavery, transferring players or buying players here and there, and putting them somewhere. And we are trying now to intervene in such cases.'
Fifa president SEPP BLATTER steps into the row about Ronaldo's reported transfer from Manchester United to Real Madrid

'I have never said that Ronaldo is a slave.'
SEPP BLATTER claims the press have distorted his words

'I think there are very few people who have really got the tradition of the club at heart. You can name them on one hand. Actually I can't name them on one hand and that's a great pity.'

Arsenal chairman PETER HILL-WOOD on players chasing big wages

'Nowadays, a lot of people sign four-year contracts and you heave a sigh of relief. Six months later they come marching in saying they want double the wages.'

Arsenal chairman PETER HILL–WOOD

'When I first started I had a club car – a Ford Escort 1.1 Mexico – but as soon as I could I bought my dream car, a BMW 3 Series. I've had a few since then. I bought Porsches and Ferraris, clothes and booze. These days I spend my money on my house, holidays and school fees.'

RYAN GIGGS

'Managers could wind you up verbally and give you a rollicking if you weren't performing and threaten to leave you out by dropping you, now you can't raise your voice to a footballer because of the immense money they're on.'

MICKY QUINN

'Obviously we get well paid, but what really counts is how many medals you finish up with, how many big games you've played in and how many experiences you can look back on at the end of your career and show your kids and grandkids.' STEVEN GERRARD

WAGS

'After the match, I went down to the tunnel and walked out on to the pitch. When I saw Geoff, I gave him a hug and a kiss and said congratulations to their manager Alf [Ramsey]. He said, which was typical of him, "It wasn't me, it was the lads." After the match we ate separately. We didn't complain – in those days, as wives, you just did what you were told.'

JUDITH HURST, wife of Geoff, on the post-match celebrations after England's World Cup win in 1966

'Footballers' wives are just as bad as benefit scroungers. These women have nannies, they don't cook or clean and never do a day's work. What kind of aspiration is that?'

CHERYL COLE

'Most people take one look at me and think, "Bimbo". It may be true that the only time I don't wear heels is to walk the dog, but my brain is just fine, thanks.'

SARAH ADAMS-LIPA, wife of Austrian international Andreas Lipa

'Priorities have changed in football and players are dictated to by their wives.'

ROY KEANE

'It was really Cathy's idea.'

SIR ALEX FERGUSON on his wife's influence in his decision not to retire

'You can go, but I'm staying here.'
RAFAEL BENITEZ on how his wife, Montse, responded to rumours he may join Real Madrid

'Yes, but what do you do for a living?'
ADRIANA SKLENARIKOVA recalls her response when Christian Karembeu told her he was a footballer

'I could lose Teddy [Sheringham] if I don't quit junk food and hit the weights.'
DANIELLE LLOYD, who did lose Teddy after appearing on *Celebrity Big Brother*

'My Sven is anything but a Swede. He seems a Sicilian. He's mega-jealous.'
NANCY DELL'OLIO

'Steven's disciplined, so I do the partying.'
ALEX CURRAN, wife of Steven Gerrard

'Apparently, more young women are getting into debt because they shop like a footballer's wife. If I heard of anyone doing that, I'd tell them to get a grip.'
COLEEN McLOUGHLIN

'The galacticos were all very different, once you got to know them. Zinedine Zidane is very quiet, family-orientated, didn't really socialize or go out. Ronie [Ronaldo] is a party animal. He was separating from his wife when we met. He's a lovely, genuine, kind person who has this phenomenal talent. Figo is charming, intelligent and a great family man. Everyone was down-to-earth. There were no egos or bodyguards.'
VICTORIA McMANAMAN

'You can be out for a quiet meal with your hubby and they come up and proffer a piece of flesh for them to sign. Then they sidle up again, drop their telephone number in his pocket and you are sitting there with him. I hate to think what happens when you are not there.'

SHELLEY WEBB, wife of Neil Webb

'I kept thinking of the legend of King Arthur, whose queen, Guinevere, fell in love with Sir Lancelot.'

NANCY DELL-OLIO on her relationship with Sven-Goran Eriksson

'He's like a second wife.'
BENNI McCARTHY on his relationship with Blackburn Rovers strike partner Jason Roberts

'I told them to go home, look at their wives and children and say, "How do you think your daddy played today?" I won't be able to look my family in the eye after that.'
STUART 'PSYCHO' PEARCE

'I know we're meant to be these hard-hearted, money-obsessed professionals but we're still little boys at heart. Just ask our wives.'
ROB LEE

'John Bond has blackened my name with his insinuations about the private lives of football managers. Both my wives are upset.'
MALCOLM ALLISON

'I will bed David Beckham.'
SUPERWAG NURIA BERMUDEZ, who boasts she has slept with the whole Real Madrid first team

'I was very surprised even though I'm from Transylvania.'
LAURA ANDRESAN, ex-*Penthouse* model, on Adrian Mutu's predilection for drinking blood

'If I'm honest, we became a bit of a circus in terms of the whole WAG situation.'
RIO FERDINAND remembers the England camp at World Cup 2006

'The best thing for a player in their football life is to have a good wife. If a player has a good wife, you don't need to worry about him.'
LUIZ FELIPE SCOLARI

'Beckham thought that a celebrity lifestyle, being drawn increasingly into the showbiz world of wife Victoria, was compatible with the regime of a professional footballer. His manager did not.'
BOBBY CHARLTON

'I was talking to Gordon Ramsay and David about this the other day, and they're the same. Gordon visualizes a meal, then figures out how to prepare it. David visualizes the goal. I'll lie in bed and think, what kind of look do I want to go for tomorrow? Then I find the pieces in my mind to create it.'
VICTORIA BECKHAM extols the virtues of 'visualization'

WEST BROMWICH ALBION

'I went in and told them that they didn't deserve to be losing 3–2 and that there was no reason in the world why we should not grab an equalizer. They all just sat there and looked at me like I was mad. Then Tony Brown said, "Boss, it's 3–3. I have just equalized."'

RON ATKINSON remembers his half-time team talk at Old Trafford in 1978

'We had some quite hostile receptions – it was extremely unpleasant. When we were going to games, you could see the National Front outside, handing out their racist literature. We never felt intimidated by it. If anything, it galvanized us into even better performances.'

BRENDAN BATSON remembers racism at football grounds in the late 1970s

'I look at the way Arsenal play now and think that's the way that we used to knock it about.'

RON ATKINSON on the ability of West Brom in the late 1970s

'It helped to break down barriers and those myths that black players had no temperament and no bottle. Watching Albion, people realized black players could play in any position.'

CYRILLE REGIS on the 'Three Degrees'

'Once you've seen one wall, you've seen them all.'

JOHN TREWICK is underwhelmed by the Great Wall of China on a club tour

'No one wanted to play against him, not even in training.'

TONY BROWN on Graham Williams

WEST HAM

'Bobby Moore was the pinnacle of everything, the one man all the other players looked up to. He personified everything that was good about the club. He had grace, mobility, humility and a fantastic technical ability as well as sportsmanship, and all these attributes were drilled into us from an early age.'

ALVIN MARTIN on Bobby Moore

'I tape over most of the player videos with *Corrie* or *Neighbours*. Most of them are crap. They can f***ing make anyone look good. I signed Marco Boogers off a video. He was a good player but a nutter. They didn't show that on the video.'

HARRY REDKNAPP

'Let's go out there to win and to win in style.'
RON GREENWOOD

'The cornerstone of my teams at West Ham for 15 years.'
JOHN LYALL on Frank Lampard, Billy Bonds and Trevor Brooking

'I've seen better fights at a wedding.'
HARRY REDKNAPP on a training ground bust-up between Alvin Martin and Matthew Rush

'It was surreal to think I played for the youth team at the start of the season and ended it in the FA Cup Final.'
17-year-old PAUL ALLEN becomes the youngest player to appear at Wembley

'The Hammers' way of playing, I think they call it the Academy these days, is all down to Ron. He introduced it, and all these years later they are still trying to play that way – I think that would have made him very happy.'

MARTIN PETERS remembers Ron Greenwood

'It's bollocks. Mind you, we had the get-out option of passing back to the goalkeeper, which would give you a breather. You could kill ten minutes that way.'

BILLY BONDS rejects the idea that 21st-century players are fitter

'As I got closer to the goal, it seemed to get smaller and smaller and Pat Jennings in goal got bigger and bigger.'

PAUL ALLEN on his run on goal at Wembley 1980 prior to being tripped by Arsenal's Willie Young

'It is a cruel game and we were outstanding. We had to dig deep, but we just couldn't dig deep enough.'

TEDDY SHERINGHAM after losing on penalties in the 2006 FA Cup Final

'Even when they had Moore, Hurst and Peters, West Ham's average finish was about 17th. It just shows how crap the other eight of us were.'

HARRY REDKNAPP on his playing days

'It was given to me by my room-mate, Keith Robson. He was always stepping over me as I was lying on the floor watching TV. Then the name stuck because of my long legs which could nick the ball away. Even now people still call me Stretch.'
ALVIN MARTIN on his nickname

'They said he couldn't run, but he was rarely beaten to the ball. They said that he couldn't jump, but he was rarely beaten in the air.'
SIR GEOFF HURST on Bobby Moore

'The best 17-year-old I've seen.'
RON GREENWOOD on Clyde Best

'I was scorned this week for saying I hated Big Brother.'
ROB GREEN at the training ground

'I knew he was going to be something, but it was not necessarily going to be a footballer.'

JOYE MANYAN, Rio Ferdinand's primary school teacher

'One bloke sat next to the dugout and kept shouting at Lee Chapman. "We haven't got Chapman again have we, Harry? He's rubbish, get rid of him." I'd used all my subs so I said, "Oi, big mouth, can you play as good as you talk?" He said, "I'm better than that effing Chapman." So I told him he was playing. We got him some boots because he didn't have any. He had West Ham tattoos all over him: legs, arms, ears. I stuck him on as centre-forward... he ran about and scored a goal. He came off and said, "I told you I was better than Chapman." He loved it and it made his day.'
HARRY REDKNAPP recalls a pre-season match at Oxford United

WOLVES

'Perhaps we should go to Ironbridge and find a 14-year-old who'll clean boots, sweep up leaves and become the greatest player in England.'

SIR JACK HAYWARD on the remote possibility of finding the next Billy Wright

'Opposition fans may sing, "Turnip, turnip, give us a wave", and the answer to that is to oblige them. I've never had a problem with the vegetable thing.'

Wolves manager GRAHAM TAYLOR is happy to answer critics of his time with England

'There they are, the champions of the world.'

STAN CULLIS hails his players following the 3–2 defeat of Honved in 1954. The Hungarian national side had defeated England the previous year

'He was an inspiring figure on the field and had a great international record. He always had time for the younger players. I never once heard him swear.'

BILL SLATER on Billy Wright

'Oh sod it, I've been here nine years – why move?'

STEVE BULL turns down Coventry City

'Wolves in those days stood for everything that was good about British football. They played with great power, spirit and style.'

SIR MATT BUSBY remembers the 1950s

'I was a different personality to David Beckham but it was a similar situation. I was never off TV, I was writing for a national newspaper, I was captain of my country, I was running the players' union and I never had to ask permission about anything.'

DEREK DOUGAN

'Luckily the sandwiches we served at lunchtime were even worse than usual. I think they had been made three weeks before and it put them off.'

SIR JACK HAYWARD on resisting the advances of foreign owners at Molineux

'It was terrific to play under floodlights, which were still primitive in those days. We had to wear plastic shirts, like those yellow jerkins police officers wear. They helped the TV cameras pick out the players, but they didn't half make you sweat. You would be wringing wet.'

RON FLOWERS

'Supporters became accustomed to free spending but, in truth, we were haemorrhaging money. That's why Sir Jack called himself "the Golden Tit".
Managing director JOHN RICHARDS on the financial situation at the club

'You don't get marks for artistic performance, do you? We had 19 clean sheets last year, played what I believe was good football and finished seventh. So I don't measure "good football".' MICK McCARTHY

WORLD CUP

'Men will be able to meet in confidence without hatred in their hearts and without an insult on their lips.'

The founding father of the World Cup, JULES RIMET, on the healing powers of football

---

'The boys call me Valderrama but I feel more like Val Doonican.'

Ireland's ANDY TOWNSEND has a bad hair day

'Thanks for the own goal.'

Reputedly shouted by the murderers of Colombian defender ANDRES ESCOBAR after he had returned home from USA 1994

'Today, God is a Bulgarian.'

HRISTO STOICHKOV is tired and emotional after victory

'It's not the sex that tires out young footballers. It's staying up all night looking for it.'

CLEMENS WESTERHOF, Nigeria's coach

'Materazzi really put on a great show when he fell down – we know how these things work.'

France coach RAYMOND DOMENECH after Zinedine Zidane was sent off in the World Cup final

'Zidane can decide a game. When the ball goes to his feet it doesn't cry – when it goes to my feet it cries.'
Portugal manager LUIZ FELIPE SCOLARI

'I just want to say sorry to all the fans. I feel as if I have let people down. I thought he miskicked the free kick and I misjudged it.'
DAVID SEAMAN on Ronaldinho's free-kick winner for Brazil in 2002

'My record of 13 goals in the World Cup finals still stands. I think I'll take it to my grave.'
JUST FONTAINE

'Kahn apart, you could take all of them, put them in a bag and hit them with a stick. Whoever got hit would deserve it.'
FRANZ BECKENBAUER on Germany's 2002 World Cup performances

'Ninety minutes before a game there is not much a coach can do. You can't talk to players, so you sit drinking tea.'
SVEN-GORAN ERIKSSON

'I am upset by Fifa's stupidity. I consider ephedrine a medicine, and I take it every day to be at my best for my public.'
Opera legend LUCIANO PAVAROTTI defends Diego Maradona after the Argentinian skipper is sent home for failing a drugs test

'*Ronaldo was scared about what lay ahead. The pressure had got to him and he couldn't stop crying. If anything, it got worse because, at about four o'clock, he started being sick. That's when I called the team doctor...*'

ROBERTO CARLOS, Ronaldo's room-mate at France 98

'**Gazza was blubbing, and Bobby was just telling me keep an eye on him. I was just repeating that back. Gazza rallied and was great in extra-time, but we were unlucky.**'

England striker GARY LINEKER recalls the semi-final defeat by Germany at Italia 90

'*It's just nice to finally put the memory of four years ago to rest.*'

DAVID BECKHAM scores a penalty in Sapporo to defeat Argentina

'*At the time people said I should have just gone through him. But I couldn't. I was going for the ball.*'

England goalkeeper PETER SHILTON on Maradona's 'Hand of God' goal

'*We were expecting Winston Churchill and instead got Iain Duncan Smith.*'

England defender GARETH SOUTHGATE on manager Sven-Goran Eriksson's half-time talk against Brazil

'*This little fellow is my last friend in the world.*'

Scotland manager ALLY MACLEOD attempts to bond with a stray dog after Scotland draw with Iran in 1978. The dog bit him

XTRA TIME

'I do want to play the short ball and I do want to play the long ball. I think long and short balls is what football is all about.' BOBBY ROBSON

'Five days shalt thou labour, as the Bible says. The seventh day is the Lord thy God's. The sixth day is for football.'

ANTHONY BURGESS

'There is no pressure at the top. The pressure's being second or third.'
JOSE MOURINHO

'I thought Borat was Man Of The Match.'
FRANK MCAVENNIE on Celtic versus St Mirren. He meant Boruc

'If you can't stand the heat in the dressing room, get out of the kitchen.'
TERRY VENABLES

'I couldn't be more chuffed if I was a badger at the start of the mating season.'
IAN HOLLOWAY

'Viv Anderson has pissed a fatness test.'
JOHN HELM

'The one great thing about football is that whatever happens it will manifest itself on the pitch. If it's right, you'll see it on the pitch, if it's wrong, it will be on the pitch. In business you can get fellas who are doing crooked deals and nobody knows anything about it. There is an ultimate honesty about football. In football you can hide for a while, but ultimately the truth comes out. I always loved that.' *JOHNNY GILES*

'I explained to him a few things about when he is running and reaches top speed, he starts to tip over – he always does that.'

USAIN BOLT on Ronaldo's tendency to fall over

'They used to be my Kevin Keegans, they went on to be my Gazzas and now they're my Rooneys.'
DAME HELEN MIRREN on her bizarre nicknames for her 'musclebound' legs

'You're just a s**t Chas and Dave.'
SPURS FANS' CHANT about Oasis when they spot Liam Gallagher in his executive box at White Hart Lane

'It would probably be the best year of my career without a shadow of a doubt to win the league and win the World Cup.'
STEVEN GERRARD tempts fate, looking forward to 2010

'He's got some facial burns but he should be okay.'
WALTER SMITH on defender Kirk Broadfoot, who poached two eggs in the microwave. One of them exploded, sending boiling water over his face

'We've been playing for an hour, and it's just occurred to me that we're drawing 0–0 with a mountain-top.'
IAN ARCHER on Scotland v San Marino

'Don't be lazy – a mixer doesn't whip as good as oneself.'
PAOLO DI CANIO on the secret of good tiramisu

'You score goals as a kid. Then you grow up stupid and become a goalkeeper.'
GIANLUIGI BUFFON

'Leaving Manchester United, in football terms, is like falling off the end of a cliff.'
GARY NEVILLE

'One door closes... another smashes you in the face!'
TOMMY DOCHERTY

'I think having Wasps around here as well gives us that little buzz around the place.'
RAY WILKINS on the Wasps–QPR groundshare

'Over the years I have heard just about every excuse that a player can use for turning up late to training. This week, however, one prominent member of the Notts County squad came up with the explanation that his electric gates were not functioning and he had to wait until the gardener turned up with the key to open it manually.'
GAVIN STRACHAN

'He took off his jacket and in one movement flung it on to a peg. I didn't even know the peg was there, so how did he? You could feel the electricity.'

JOHN ROBERTSON on Brian Clough's arrival at Forest

'Although I am not a vain person I believe I am the best footballer in the whole world.'

RONALDINHO

'Last year's race was a bit of a damp squid.'

MARK HATELEY on the Scottish title

'Carlton covers every blade of grass on the pitch... but then you have to if your first touch is that crap.'

DAVE JONES on Carlton Palmer

'I am no longer a footballer. I am an industry.'

JOHAN CRUYFF

'Alan Shearer is arguably the best footballer this country has ever produced. I don't think anyone can argue with that.'

DANNY HIGGINBOTHAM

'The Albanians are penetrating us from all positions.'

NIALL QUINN

'As soon as he died I was receiving thousands of letters that were just addressed to Mrs Bobby Moore, England.'
STEPHANIE MOORE on the death of the England legend

'I loved football. I played in the morning and in the afternoon. Even when I went to bed with my wife, I was training.'
DIEGO MARADONA

'I went into the club shop to get the T-shirt two or three days after they'd gone on sale but they had already sold out.'
JOHN JENSEN on the commemorative shirt printed after he scored his one and only Arsenal goal

'I'm so glad there will now be two good-looking guys at Real. I've felt so lonely in such an ugly team.'
ROBERTO CARLOS on hearing Beckham is coming to the Bernabeu

'I tried to get the disappointment out of my system by going for a walk. I ended up 17 miles from home and I had to phone my wife Lesley to come and pick me up.'
GORDON STRACHAN after losing to Everton

'Logically, anyway, Arsenal should prosper at the Emirates. No side in the Premiership is so reliant for success on passing and movement, on the creation of space, and there is, quite simply, more space at the new ground. The pitch there was notoriously small, measuring just 101m by 67m – Wenger once even used the lack of space to explain why his sides picked up so many bookings. At the new ground the pitch measures 113m by 76m, an additional 1821m².'
JONATHAN WILSON

'The more money that comes into football the more of a buzz it will give the gangsters to be involved. To my knowledge there are current Premier League players who are friends with gangsters. There are certain individuals that will be getting looked after – by that I mean if players are in any trouble they know the right people to go to. It will be a rare day that a Premier League player can go from morning to night and not be introduced to, or speak to, somebody who's involved in the drugs trade or some other form of criminality.'

MARK WARD, ex-Everton and West Ham winger, who was jailed when cocaine with a street value of £645,000 was found at a house he had rented

'You felt this was the sort of game that needed a goal to break the deadlock.'
RON JONES

'He has magnificent qualities, although after today's assault on him, he may well want to go back to the tranquil life of Bordeaux.'

STEVE BRUCE after Christophe Dugarry encounters Blackburn Rovers for the first time

'Mark Hughes is playing better and better, even if he is going grey and looking like a pigeon.'

GIANLUCA VIALLI

'No cheating bastards will I talk to; I will not talk to any cheating bastards!'

BRIAN CLOUGH giving the Italian press the cold shoulder after losing to Juventus

'The first 90 minutes of the match are the most important.'

BOBBY ROBSON